Transnational Feminism and Global Advocacy in South Asia

Transnational feminism has been critical to feminist theorizing in the global North over the last few decades. Perhaps due to its broad terminology, transnational feminism can become vague and dislocated, losing its ability to name specific critiques of and responses to empire, race, and globalization that are emboldened by its transnational remit. This volume encompasses an expansive engagement and exploration of transnational South Asian feminist movements, networks, and critiques within the context of the popular and the diaspora in South Asia. The contributing authors address key issues in a global context, especially as they operate both in a situated and the diasporic imaginary of South Asia.

While the idea of the popular in South Asia has often been circumscribed by the spaces and cultural politics of Bollywood, this interdisciplinary volume takes an innovative turn to examine how academics, advocates, activists, and artists envision the inroads and consequences of nationalism, globalization and/or empire, which continually remake communities and alter needs and allegiances. Through ethnography, literature, dance, cinema, activism, poetry, and storytelling, the authors analyse popular and social justice using a focused, multidisciplinary gendered lens.

This book was originally published as a special issue of *South Asian Popular Culture.*

Gita Rajan is Professor of English and a Senior Research Fellow at the Center for Faith and Public Life at Fairfield University, USA. Her research interests include South Asian literature and visual culture, feminist ethics, and advocacy models for sustainable globalization.

Jigna Desai is Associate Professor in the Department of Gender, Women, and Sexuality Studies and Asian American Studies Program at the University of Minnesota, USA. Her research interests include Asian American, postcolonial, queer, disability, and diasporic cultural studies.

Transnational Feminism and Global Advocacy in South Asia

Edited by
Gita Rajan and Jigna Desai

Routledge
Taylor & Francis Group
LONDON AND NEW YORK

First published 2013
by Routledge
2 Park Square, Milton Park, Abingdon, Oxon, OX14 4RN

Simultaneously published in the USA and Canada
by Routledge
711 Third Avenue, New York, NY 10017

Routledge is an imprint of the Taylor & Francis Group, an informa business

This book is a reproduction of *South Asian Popular Culture*, volume 8, issue 1. The Publisher requests to those authors who may be citing this book to state, also, the bibliographical details of the special issue on which the book was based.

British Library Cataloguing in Publication Data
A catalogue record for this book is available from the British Library

ISBN13: 978-0-415-50385-3

Typeset in Times New Roman
by Taylor & Francis Books

Publisher's Note
The publisher would like to make readers aware that the chapters in this book may be referred to as articles as they are identical to the articles published in the special issue. The publisher accepts responsibility for any inconsistencies that may have arisen in the course of preparing this volume for print.

Printed and bound in the United States of America by Publishers Graphics, LLC on sustainably sourced paper.

Contents

Notes on Contributors

Ananya Chatterjea is a dancer, choreographer, dance scholar, and dance educator, who envisions her work in the field of dance as a 'call to action' with a particular focus on women artists of color. She is the Artistic Director of Ananya Dance Theatre, a company of women artists of color committed to the intersection of artistic excellence and social justice (www.ananyadancetheatre.org). She is also Director of Dance and Professor in the Department of Theater Arts and Dance at the University of Minnesota, Minneapolis, USA. Her most recent choreographic project, 'Ashesh Barsha, unending monsoon, the culmination of a trilogy on environmental justice', premiered in Minneapolis' Southern Theater, in September 2009. Her book, *Butting out! Reading cultural politics in the work of Chandralekha and Jawole Willa Jo Zollar*, was published by Wesleyan University Press in 2004.

Piya Chatterjee is Dorothy Cruickshank Backstrand Chair at the Department of Women and Gender Studies, Scripps College, Claremont, CA, USA. She is author of *A Time for Tea: Women Labor and Post/Colonial Politics on an Indian Plantation* (Duke, 2001) and co-editor (with Manali Desai and Parama Roy) of *States of Trauma: Gender and Violence in South Asia* (Zubaan, 2010). She is also the editor of a series at the University of Illinois Press, *Dissident Feminisms.* She lives bi-nationally and is involved in antiviolence organizing with rural plantation and village women in eastern India.

Jigna Desai is an associate professor in the Department of Gender, Women, and Sexuality Studies and the Asian American Studies Program at the University of Minnesota. Her research interests include feminist science and disability, Asian American, postcolonial, queer, and diasporic cultural studies. Her book *Beyond Bollywood: The Cultural Politics of South Asian Diasporic Film* is the first book on media and the South Asian diaspora. It analyzes the complex gender and racial politics of diasporas in the current moment of globalization (Routledge 2004). She is the co-editor of a collection entitled *Bollywood: A Reader* for Open University /McGraw Hill Press (2009) and for *Asian Americans Down South: Race and Migration in Dixie* forthcoming with the Univ. of Illinois Press. She has published widely on issues of race, media, gender, and sexuality in numerous international anthologies and journals such as *Social Text, Journal of Asian American Studies,* and *Meridiens.* Her current research is on neurodiversity, autism, and the globalization of disability.

R. Diyah Larasati is Assistant Professor of Theatre Arts & Dance at the University of Minnesota, USA. She explores in her advocacy/activist project, 'Choreographing

History', the archiving of female dancing bodies in colonial reports and how moral codes stigmatize racialized, colonized bodies. She collaborates with Indonesian choreographer Setyastuti, and is supported by grants, including the Consortium Study of the Asias (2009), Office of International Programs (2008), the McKnight Travel Grant (2007), and Center for History and Political Ethic/PUSDEP Sanatadharma Indonesia, to create performances based on the oral history of Indonesian female dancers who are the survivors of the horrible genocide.

Sunaina Maira is Professor of Asian American Studies at the University of California, Davis, USA. She is the author of *Desis in the House: Indian American Youth Culture in New York City* and co-editor of *Youthscapes: The Popular, the National, the Global and Contours of the Heart: South Asians Map North America*, which won the American Book Award in 1997. Her most recent book, *Missing: Youth, Citizenship, and Empire After 9/11* (Duke University Press, 2009), is on South Asian Muslim immigrant youth in the US and issues of citizenship and empire after 9/11.

Richa Nagar is Professor of Gender, Women and Sexuality Studies at the University of Minnesota, USA, and a member of Sangtin Kisaan Mazdoor Sangathan in Sitapur, India. She co-authored *Sangtin Yatra: Saat Zindagiyon mein Lipta Nari Vimarsh, Playing with Fire: Feminist Thought and Activism through Seven Lives in India, A World of Difference: Encountering and Contesting Development* and co-edited *Critical Transnational Feminist Studies.* Richa's academic research on gender, race, and communal politics among South Asian communities in postcolonial Tanzania and her subsequent work have resulted in numerous articles. Since 1996, her research, organizing, and creative work in Hindustani have focused mainly on collaborative efforts that seek to reconfigure the political terrain and processes associated with 'empowerment' projects aimed at 'the poor.'

Rani Neutill has been an Andrew W. Mellon Postdoctoral Fellow in the Department of English at Johns Hopkins University and a Postdoctoral Associate in the Program in Ethnicity, Race and Migration at Yale University, USA. She is working on a manuscript entitled *'Intimacies of Hatred'* that rethinks the idea of 'South Asian American Literature' by examining diasporic writers who reconceptualize the categories of nation and home through representations of the exile and violence associated with the Partition of India.

Gita Rajan is Professor of English and Senior Research Fellow at the Center for Faith and Public Life at Fairfield University, USA. She was an Andrew Mellon Fellow at University of Pennsylvania, a Paul Mellon Fellow at the British Center of Art at Yale University, a Scholar in Residence at New York University, and a Visiting Endowed Chair of Women's Studies at Hamilton College. Her research and publication interests include gender and development, feminist ethics, South Asian literature and visual culture, and serving as an advocate for women in sustainable globalization, especially through her work on the Connecticut Council of Vital Voices Global Partnership. Her last edited anthology, *New Cosmopolitanisms: South Asians in the US* was published by Stanford University Press.

Shreen Saroor is an activist and founder of Mannar Women Development Federation that addresses the needs of war affected women. She was an Echoing Green Fellow and part of the woman peacemakers program of John B. Kroc Institute for Peace and Justice, San Diego California. Currently she heads the Ashoka Innovators for the Public office in Sri Lanka.

Kumarini Silva is Assistant Professor of Communication Studies at Northeastern University in Boston, USA. Her research interrogates the intersection between diaspora, immigration, and popular culture.

Richa Singh, a founding member of Sangtin Kisaan Mazdoor Sangathan in Sitapur, India, stepped into the world of activism in 1991 as a member of the office staff at Mahila Samakhya Programme (MS) in Banaras and later emerged as a mobilizer and district coordinator in the Saharanpur and Sitapur programs of MS. In MS, Richa participated in critical dialogues on violence against women and on formal and informal education on regional and national platforms. The co-authorship and publication of *Sangtin Yatra: Saat Zindagiyon mein Lipta Nari Vimarsh* in 2004 gave Richa a new direction, and marked the beginning of her full-time immersion in movement-building with the peasants and workers of Sitapur District to build and strengthen Sangtin Kisaan Mazdoor Sangathan, which currently focuses on issues such as access to irrigation waters, livelihoods, land redistribution, and caste and gender violence.

Transnational feminism and global advocacy in South Asia

Gita Rajan and Jigna Desai

This collection presents South Asian and diasporic strands of transnational feminism that intermingle with the forces of globalization and empire and that are strategically deployed using models of advocacy and activism. The scholars in this collection explore how a series of existing and emerging feminist ideas and theories address, intersect, and measure-up against development goals, empowerment work, and post-colonial representations in South Asia and its diasporas. Together, the essays examine the multiplicity of modes through which academics, activists, advocates, Non Governmental Organization (NGO) workers, and artists, often in collaboration with people on the ground, articulate relations of power, advocate for subjects, and envision and remake communities. Both the issues they write about and the sites they operate in are useful in contesting and re-imagining ways of knowing and being within South Asia and its diasporas. Hence, a thematic strain in this anthology is a scrutiny of factors and agents that inhibit and create transformations in the experiential realities and lived imaginaries of South Asian people, both rooted and diasporic. This insistence on capturing the broad brush-strokes as well as the fine nuances of circumstances of situated and diasporic peoples is to signal how conditioned both are by a wide range of global forces, and consequently, how they are mutually, albeit unevenly interrelated and inclusive. Our goal is to highlight such spaces or more accurately gesture to connections that function as localized zones, as intersecting points, as links and networks, and as places that activate transnational and global momentum to theorize new visions of community formations grounded upon social justice. The deliberate breach of discourse categories (or genre boundaries) in this volume, ranging from theoretical and personal reflections to literary analysis and ethnographic accounts, is an attempt to capture trajectories of global forces playing out in actual spaces, and trace sites where transformative opportunities can occur. The potential of such transformations is the ability to translate change to signal social justice for the people across multiple venues.

Transnational Feminism

Posed as an alternative to international and global feminisms as well as a means to address gender within a shifting, differential global context, transnational feminism as a site of theory and praxis has burgeoned within the last few decades. Arguing against a global sisterhood *and* the siloing off of feminisms within state territorial boundaries, transnational feminism has emerged as a predominant way to understand processes at a scale smaller and larger than the nation-state. Within this context, scholars have insisted upon transnational feminism's supple abilities to address a host of growing concerns including empire, nationalism, race, capitalism, war, neoliberalism, and state violence. Often seen as incorporating other feminisms such as postcolonial and Third World feminisms within its rubric, transnational feminism has become central to feminist interrogations of globalization, empire, and the nation-state in the global North and South. Suffice to say, rather than suggesting some universal category of gender and woman at its foundation, transnational feminism has sought to articulate the gendered impact of a wide range of global processes and forces within their particular geopolitical contexts.

Transnational feminist scholarship is frequently positioned at a generalized theoretical level that signals the global, but then functions as an analysis by proxy of specific, national and local particularities. In light of long deliberations about its domains, scope, and location, it is now time to consider *specific* iterations of transnational feminism. This is to say that transnational feminisms are neither general and universal nor only particular and local. We can understand transnational feminism in its many distinguishable formations. Straddling regions, networks, and diasporas, manifestations of transnational feminism, such as transnational South Asian feminism, may function as particular yet partly ambiguous iterations of what we now call transnational feminism. We argue that it may be appropriate to identify distinctive manifestations of transnational feminism that are both generalized and particular in order to build more specific and rich theorizations of feminism. Transnational South Asian feminism(s) can be seen as epistemic and geopolitical formulations constituted by multiple nodes located within the region of South Asia and its diasporas.

South Asia as a region evokes the prolonged history of area studies. While South Asia is understood as a region within the context of Cold War era area studies, scholars from the global South have used the term to designate their own understanding of this geopolitical space with related, if not intersecting, concerns. This collection of essay emerges from a special issue of *South Asian Popular Culture,* a journal that very consciously locates itself transnationally while theorizing and negotiating the complexity of the region of South Asia and its diasporas. Clearly, the essays featured here reflect a similar engagement with South Asia, even as they replicate the general academic and activist geopolitical bias towards India and production from within the US academy. While it is accurate to state that many of the essays herein are accounts of how transnational feminist principles and/or theories function within local frameworks, and many of these incentives have activist aspirations, the work of these scholars signal the potential to be extrapolated and to engage in advocacy discussions.

South Asian feminism has focused on a constellation of concerns engendered by the South Asian histories of colonialism, nationalism, war, caste, global capitalism, and/or religious hegemony. This volume more narrowly offers several perspectives on transnational South Asian feminism as a method for addressing issues of global advocacy, gender, and social justice. We hope that this collection is timely in imagining some of the terrain of transnational South Asian feminisms as few scholarly books offer such a focus, especially within a global context. Of course, this modest set of essays cannot ensure coverage of South Asian feminisms, if there were such a thing. Instead, specific transnational South Asian feminisms are implicitly and explicitly delineated through engagements with various concerns recognized under the rubric of transnational South Asian feminism. Within this collection, South Asian feminism is neither singularly coherent nor distinctively fixed. Each of the scholars here understands transnational South Asian feminism differently as she highlights different concerns and conversations extend South Asian feminism beyond the nation and region. While some consider racialization and empire, war and NGOization, or the trauma of Partition, others evoke diasporic, North-South, or women of color collaborations in their commitment to the transnational. If anything as we are forced to consider the numerous facets of transnational South Asian feminism – those that address globalization, empire, nationalism, war, and NGOization, – it is clear that there cannot be a singularity of meaning, but instead an interrelated constellation of concerns. In fact, transnational South Asian feminisms forge and maintain conversations that bridge these concerns within the region and beyond.

In charting South Asian feminism through nodes of connectivity, we understand transnational feminisms as specific but unfixed formations of material networks and epistemic clusters. These nodes constitute the region beyond geopolitical territories and nation states, and demand that we participate with responsible attentiveness to the multiple iterations of transnational South Asian feminism.

Global Advocacy

Over the last three decades or so, even as the sheer number of people speaking about the nature, significance, and impact of globalization has increased exponentially, the discussions themselves have remained discrete and guided by disciplinary premises, albeit with a few infrequent overlaps amongst the discussants and their viewpoints. And, even as we seem to privilege the paths that global forces take, we are cognizant (as our authors here) of the fact that the postcolonial predicament is very real for many peoples of South Asia, as are the advantages and disadvantages that diasporic agents bring to bear on national and transnational questions. Highlighting global forces thus help us mark a contemporary moment in understanding how gender advocacy operates in a transnational context, and equally important, what aspects of that advocacy are powered by what are articulated as local interests, and what issues seem worth exploring for migrant populations. While it is accurate to state that many of the essays herein are accounts of how transnational feminist principles and/or theories function within local frameworks, and many of these incentives have activist aspirations and groundings, the work of these scholars signal the potential to be extrapolated and to engage in advocacy discussions as well.

To advocate means to speak in support of, usually in relation to the law. Coming from the Latin, *advocātus*, to call someone to one's aid, was used within the context of seeking justice in court. To advocate implies to speak in relation to the authority of the law on behalf of either oneself or who one who cannot adequately speak for herself. This collection proposes that transnational feminist advocacy extends beyond the court of law to seek and define alternative sites of justice. In fact, feminist scholars have indicated the significant rise of transnational advocacy networks that cross state borders via NGOs and development capital that are now themselves critical actors within global civil society. Transnational networks engage appeals for justice across state and other borders to address globalization and other national and transnational processes. Transnational Feminist Networks (TFNs) generally pursue justice (whether gender, economic, social, or restorative) within the context of feminism itself, especially in development issues via alternative institutional structures such as NGOs and Community Based Organizations (CBOs).

This collection understands transnational feminist advocacy to be firmly grounded within these institutional and discursive locations, but also returns to the centrality of the insistent *vox* (voice) integral to advocacy. In other words, questions of voice and representation critical to advocacy are presented within this collection through an engagement with popular culture. The stories, testimonies, narratives, images, and memories that advocate for justice here identify and refuse to resolve questions of voice within the context of feminist networks. Instead, their transnational feminist engagements with popular culture address the complexities of border-crossing knowledges within globalization.

This collection approaches global advocacy in ways that trouble the authority and legitimacy afforded to policy analysis and ethnography (despite the self-critique of ethnographers) as the best methods to deliver transparent knowledge of the other within the global South. Clearly, the activists and scholars here methodologically approach knowledge and globalization from different vantage points. The various essays discuss and analyze aspects of interventions in feminist advocacy to illuminate a broad cross-section of South Asian feminism. Turning to analyses of academic knowledge production, imperial feminist media, ethnographic accounts, and storytelling as a mode of social movements, for example, authors in the collection present models for understanding how aesthetic efforts work in tandem with analytical research to engender transformations.

The rationale for raising the issue of both transnational feminism and social justice in the context of cultural projects within the volume is because much development work is being conducted in this terrain, extending in most nations beyond entertainment and media productions to activating global-local participation in political, cultural, economic, educational and religious realms. More than many other endeavors, development projects feed into this energy. While the initiatives undertaken in the name of development have been extremely uneven, for many feminists, it is still worth using that terminology to grasp why transnational feminism can be mobilized to engender change in the lives of the people. Not all change has been good for the peoples of South Asia, as has been amply proven by assessments of development goals, especially those powered by the global North. This statement alerts readers to our own ambivalence in discussing the impact of development programs. These programs carry with them the imprimatur of global agents and agencies whose understanding of local needs has a lot to be desired and has been brought into question by social movements and organizations themselves. And yet, many would argue that without the force of national and transnational agencies that chose to adopt and comply with the United Nations Millennium Development Goals, many of the gains made by local states and NGOs could not be sustained.

Amartya Sen makes an invaluable point that helps clarify our (the authors and perhaps feminists in general) ambivalence in broaching the usefulness of this global endeavor. In *Development as Freedom*, he writes: "Development can be seen … as a process of expanding the real freedoms that people enjoy. Focusing on human freedoms contrasts with narrower views of development, such as identifying development with the growth of gross national product, or with the rise in personal incomes, or with industrialization, or with technological advance or with social modernization. Growth of GNP or of individual incomes can, of course, be very important as means to expanding the freedoms enjoyed by all members of society. But, freedoms depend also on other determinants, such as social and economic arrangements (for example, facilities for education and health care) as well as political and civil rights (for example, the liberty to participate in public discussion and scrutiny)" (29).[1] It is noteworthy that Sen incorporates other freedoms that have to do with the possibility of women exercising rights over their own lives, their economic status, health, safety, and the education for children. And, as many of the authors here discuss, it is here that transnational feminism and global advocacy can play a meaningful role.

Women in/and globalization

Discourses about globalization generally equate globalization with global capitalism. Within global advocacy discourses, capitalism operates as the primary agent of displacements that contends with more "local" forms such as culture and kinship so that transnational economic forces work with or against local formations. Typical anti-globalization narratives of capitalism propose that global capital rides roughshod over local forms that resist with varying levels of success. Transnational Feminist Networks' discourses often frame capitalism as the singular global force that needs to be opposed by transnational feminism and gendered global advocacy. Other forces, such as war, caste-ism, and patriarchy are imagined as local phenomena, which must be accounted for, but nevertheless be subordinated to the larger significance of capitalism. Some scholars have critiqued the centrality that capitalism has been assigned within discourses on globalization arguing for nuanced and less totalizing theories of capitalism (see Mohanty, Gibson-Graham, and Grewal and Kaplan).[2] Underlying these discussions is a need to dismantle the spatial binary of global/local or even the awkward neologism glocal that is used to characterize these processes. Instead, we attempt to understand how the local and global are mutually constituted in ways that neither indicate the hegemony of the global (in the form of capital) nor the essential resistance of the local (imagined as local phenomena such as community and culture). Transnational South Asian feminism may need to develop the means to consider local, national, regional, and global simultaneously and as mutually constitutive within our analyses, theories, and praxis.

To enter into a discourse arena on globalization and culture, Marshall McLuhan's famous aphorism, *the medium is the massage* is worth considering. McLuhan intentionally allowed *massage* to be his final word (the press changed the original spelling to message), because he argues that it describes what we implicitly grasp as the large scale maneuvering of meaning in a 20th century avatar of modernity. But the strategy of managing meaning rings true of our unevenly transitioning global reality too; a condition that Arjun Appadurai describes vividly and visually as a *disjuncture. Disjuncture* is best understood as the jagged ends meshing together to mirror differentially merging realities of the nature and impact of global forces, i.e. there is a connectedness at the macro and micro levels of the causes and effects of global occurrences, which, in converse, also show fracture/stress lines at the level of macro-micro links. But massaging the message is a useful phrase to follow if we trace how and why various hypotheses about globalization are staged—ranging from media (both traditional and new), academia, novelists and playwrights, financial institutions, economic pundits, policy makers, NGOs, and of course, the state and transnational agencies—to hone in on a specific outcome. In this historical moment of a hyped-up mode of globalization each actor seizes specific messages to highlight, while taking exaggerated swipes at opposing ideas or less advantageous ones. For our purposes, *disjuncture* becomes discernible in the diverse analyses used to spotlight the complex, multi-originary, and multi-pronged trajectories that global forces have been propelled and thus resulted in very different outcomes.

For example, till very recently, development projects did not calculate or consider the strengths of local communities they worked with, i.e., a top-down approach and a needs-based formula rather than an asset-based one. Identifying this as a misstep, a whole slew of actors, including states, policy advocates, researchers, development agencies, various global entities, and beneficiaries themselves—private and public partners in this crowded world—acknowledged that there are gaps in both in the production of knowledge and data analysis. Here the *disjuncture* was between development dollars and local requirements. Disjuncture here does not suggest some kind of smoothly operating local shredded and torn asunder by the force of globalization, but rather the ways that the local was slowly incorporated into the domain of the global which itself was transformed by the processes. In other words, they localized the global as they also further disseminated its domain. This led to extremely uneven results as the primary goal of empowering peoples and communities was often unmet. This call for local needs to be incorporated systemically has led to complex processes of mediation, negotiation, and translation. Therefore, there is a growing awareness of the need to effectively address and understand inequities and injustices with a call to accountability and humane intervention as a much-needed corrective to *doing business* (corporate, state, or development) in this new century.

One particular feature in assessing the benefits and ravages of globalization has been the role that women play both wittingly and unwittingly in the process. There is a general consensus initiated by women's groups from the global South, then advanced by the managerially run NGOs in the North and South, which is now beginning to be heralded by global agencies such as the United Nations that there is a need to recognize the centrality of women's labor in all development agendas and projects. Women from the global South not only do a disproportionate part of the work of globalization, but they are also caught in the chaotic, intended and unintended machinations of global forces. Valentine Moghadam captures this succinctly: "the mid-1980s saw the formation of a number of transnational feminist networks that brought women from the developed and developing countries together … to respond to economic pressures and patriarchal movements: [namely] Development Alternatives with Women for a New Era (DAWN), Women in Development Europe (WIDE), Women Living under Muslim Laws (WLUML), and the Sisterhood is Global Institute" (8).[3] We can add Women and Development (WAD), Women in Development (WID), and UNIFEM to the list as prominent players. (This last office has now been reorganized under Michelle Bachelet as the First Under Secretary and Executive Director of UN Women.) This body's recent global meeting on the Commission on the Status of Women (in New York City from February 27 – March 9, 2012) is a case in point that illustrates the distance traveled from the time of creating awareness (Moghadam) to deploying development programs.[4] The expansion of gendered global advocacy has led to the greater integration of women's participation in state and development processes in a wide range of domains —from meeting health and nutrition needs to political and economic participation, to food and energy security, to safeguarding freedoms when persecuted by states or by religious fundamentalists, to protecting the environment—for both urban and rural women. We mention these agencies and their recent initiatives not to laud them, but to draw attention to the massive global expansion that is focused on the integration of women within development capitalism and state advocacy, which have yielded mixed results. Our focus here is to shed some light on complex global forces impacting gender dynamics in South Asia using a three step model: give a context about existing ideas and initiatives within South Asia and its diasporas, explore where transnational feminists are identifying and advocating social justice, and open up spaces for different conversations and viewpoints regarding global advocacy. Of course, we recognize that we follow a trajectory set by noted feminists, academics and advocates such as Sidonie Smith, Sandra Harding, Wendy S. Hesford, Amrita Basu, Rosi Braidotti, Carol Gould, Vandana Shiva, and Inderpal Grewal[5], to name just a few.

After several decades of scholarship and activism, it is clear that gender and globalization are pervasive issues throughout South Asia. The dissemination of capital, development, and NGOization within the context of neoliberalism and globalization has led to the increasing penetration of such economies within everyday life. To give an example from South Asia in the field of basic life security and gender equity, micro-lending has been considered a boon, but the consequent re-insertion of middle-men has made women vulnerable to sexual and economic exploitation all over again with recent reports of borrowers committing suicide, perhaps through coercion from lenders due to their inability to pay. Understanding how micro-lending has been useful to some but devastating to others requires questioning the expansion of capital occurring through NGOization and development capital in the name of women's empowerment and participation. Transnational feminist critique must be able to acknowledge both who has been enabled and who has been injured through such practices and policies.

It may be that the expansion of development capital, NGOs, and Transnational Feminist Networks has become a global economic force in which feminist organizing itself is brought further into an economy of exchange. It is worth considering if the extensiveness of NGOs and development capital has led to the increasing commodification of knowledge and interaction among feminist participants. As feminist organizing becomes further integrated into transnational networks and capital, a constant maximization of engagement in the pursuit of social and economic capital seems likely. This is not just to say that NGOs have become professionalized, but that social organizing processes themselves are becoming susceptible to commodification such that there is a value attributed to each exchange that can be transformed into professional, developmental, and academic goals. In other words, a calculus of human interaction and knowledge production that links CBOs and NGOs, universities, global actors such as the UN, and state agencies are transforming how feminist participants are accruing social and economic capital.

To understand the inherent complexity of global initiatives and their actual impact on improving women's lives from a transnational feminist perspective, Myra Marx Ferree and Aili Mari Tripp's insight is useful, albeit more academic:

> Feminist mobilizations are informed by feminist theory, beliefs, and practices, but they take place in a variety of organizational contexts within governments. Feminism as a goal often informs all or part of the agenda of mixed gender organizations. [....] Because feminism challenges all of gender relations, it also addresses those norms and processes of gender construction and oppression that differentially advantage some women and men relative to others. [....] Feminist activists and activism typically are embedded in organizations and institutions with multiple goals. To have a feminist goal is in no way inconsistent with having other political and social goals as well. The question of where feminism stands on the list of priorities of any individual or group is an empirical one. It is not true by definition that a person or group that calls itself feminist necessarily puts this particular goal in the first place, since in practice it could be discovered to be displaced by other values. [....] Nor is it true by definition that a person or group that does not call

itself feminist does not have a feminist goal, since identity can carry other connotations in local settings. (6-7).[6]

Marx Ferree and Tripp offer us cautionary advice. In discussing the complexities of how feminist activists are located within their organizational contexts, Marx Ferree and Tripp identify the possibility of privileges being accessible to only some women (and men) even within feminist organizing. But they also suggest that recognizing and attending to multiple forms of social difference is paramount within transnational feminist praxis, even to the degree that gender is subordinated to other factors. Marx Ferree and Tripp offer us the insight that even within feminist collectives, attention to multiple inequities remains a central tenet of feminist praxis.

Human Rights

More generally, within the context of South Asian feminist and progressive movements, the efficacy and promise of human rights has been brought into question and is seen sometimes as being an impasse by theorists. Academics would argue that the concept of human rights with their liberal and colonial roots continue to be attached to problematic concepts of historical progress, democracy, and equality. The question of rights themselves and women's rights in particular has been a site of interrogation within postcolonial and South Asian feminist conversations. If the category woman has been constituted in and through the figure of the racial Other, how might this give us pause in deploying women's rights within the global South? More specifically, as Diane Detournay[7] writes, the postcolonial other as savage is foundational to the category of woman and women's rights within liberalism and feminism.

"Given the global trend towards fragmentation along cultural lines, can universal human rights regimes help transcend paradoxical identity formations that subordinate women to a patriarchal gender order of competing masculinities operating locally, nationally, and internationally?"[8] One of the most ubiquitous rubrics used to hold states responsible for ensuring women's safety within gendered global advocacy discourses is that of human rights. In order to provide women in the developing world access to vital resources that is systemically denied to them because of their status as women, i.e., paternalistic kinship systems and patriarchal power systems that are a carry-over from imperial protocols, Hillary Clinton's declaration that women's rights are human rights was a cataclysmic moment in marrying the UN's Millennium Development Goals to development agendas.[9] Her statement on women's rights as well as her more recent statement about sexuality indicate the globalizing of women' s rights and sexual rights that are supported and funded by nation-states from the global North. Recognition of women's rights and, more recently, Lesbian, Gay, Bisexual, and Transgender (LGBT) rights have been understood as markers of progress towards achieving human rights within Western models of liberal democracy and progress.

It is worth turning our attention to some of the ways that human rights have been brought into question within transnational South Asian feminism. For example, the program, "Claiming our Rights: A Manual for Women's Human Rights Education in Muslim Societies," created by Sisterhood is Global Institute has had limited success in South Asia (New Delhi), as it has not diminished the atrocities and violence in Pakistan and Bangladesh, even though it has had some success in other places like the Middle East, North Africa, and Central Asia (Moghadam 158). One complexity arises when states remain silent and even tacitly sanction the violence despite the championing of universal rights and women's agency by global agencies, advocates, and transnational feminists. The situation becomes more complex when we consider the framing of human rights as normalizing discourses for marginalized subjects. For example, in the case of sexual and gender minorities (included GLBT and gender non-conforming individuals), advocacy for human rights is conflated with the Westernization, homogenization, and normalization of sexual and gender non-normativities. Some argue that certain sexual and gender identities in the global South are merely manifestations of Western capital and power. Hence, conservative and fundamentalist groups within South Asia often attempt to characterize social movements focused on gender and sexuality as Western and imperialist; this perspective has engendered the oppositional position suggesting that same sex sexualities and transgender identities in the global South are "purely" indigenous (e.g. hijra) or regional precolonial manifestations of sexualities. Which terms are recognized and whose agendas implemented are central questions faced by advocates and activists working in the global arena?

How are local, nationalist, and global discourses pressed into service to produce legible marginal subjectivities that must continue to be examined? This question is important in our global era when a subject's identity is anchored in citizenship and under scrutiny by national laws, and also simultaneously pressed upon by globalized forces of multiple kinds including corporate and development capital as well as human rights. What recourse do bodies that do not wish to be disciplined have when they access local, regional, and transnational resources? Furthermore, what kinds of geopolitical imperatives guide the work of global agencies engaged systematically in dealing with war survivors in Sri Lanka, widows in Afghanistan, or the trafficking and subjugation of women? How can they rebuild civil and civic communities that are fractured by fear, stigma, and distrust? How can they negotiate the demand to conform to legible and recognizable categories within liberalism and human rights?

What terms are appropriate and whose agendas are implemented are central questions faced by advocates working in the global arena. The speed and scale of 'NGOizaton' within all the countries in South Asia creates a different kind of problem when local traditions and cultural sensibilities are pitted against gender and sexual normativities that are viewed as the representational politics of the global North, especially in taboo areas like LGBT life and treatment of HIV/AIDS. What nationalist narratives are pressed into service to uphold binary, normative mode of marginal subjectivity that now must to be re-examined? This question is important in our global era when a subject's identity is anchored in citizenship and under scrutiny by national laws, and also simultaneously pressed upon by globalized forces of multiple kinds including transnational capitalism within corporations.

Nodes

Each of the essays locates itself in a specific node of transnational connectivity and disjuncture and allows us to address the global condition. Diyah Laraseti wrestles with how she is continually displaced from herself and her home, the latter a space that is remembered through the colonial archive, state genocide, globalized liberal feminism, and migration. From the halls of the university to popular liberal feminism, Laraseti details her encounters with the recent and rapid circulation of narrative and images produced by a predatory imperial feminism traveling through and consuming South and Southeast Asia. With sorrow, the essay calls forth across the ocean, the dancing corpses of the mass murders and genocide that haunt these celebratory landscapes of Indonesian cosmopolitanism and tradition and now the plains of the Midwest. In doing so, Laraseti's essay becomes a moment in which eating, praying, and loving is an act of feminist responsibility to and remembrance of the dead rather than refurbished imperial feminist memories of travel and leisure as so often is the case. The reification of nationalism is the subject of Rani Neutill's essay on representations of Partition as a significant node within South Asia and diasporic narratives. Her fine grain analysis of the sexualities produced and disciplined in the moment of Partition elucidates how the heterosexual rape of women becomes the singular dominant formulation of Partition. Neutill deftly cleaves a path of non-heteronormative sexualities through these Partition narratives that are produced within transnational South Asian feminist popular culture, thereby eschewing any attempt to rent asunder the postcolonial, diasporic, and global from the domain of transnational South Asian feminist and queer critique.

South Asian communities can be seen as nodes in extensive and rapidly expanding transnational networks of global migration. The working class Muslim South Asian American youth of Sunaina Maira's study constitute an ethnographic node in the web of US empire and global anti-Muslim racism. Like Laraseti, Maira insightfully allows the reader to see the disavowals of the dominant constructions of race and othering in the youths' dissenting citizenship. Savvy in their negotiations with cultural forms and racial discourses, the critical observations of the youths reverberate with those made by other Muslim anti-racist activists throughout Europe and elsewhere. Kumarini Silva's essay looks at second-generation South Asian American youth also, but from an acute perspective; she clarifies the transnational imaginings that create advocacy and activists connectivities between the diaspora in the US and India. These connections, according to Silva, are constituted by diasporic nationalism, neoliberalism, and romanticized pastoralism. Neuill and Silva albeit in different domains, elucidate how the nation is safely anchored and moored within the transnational space of diaspora.

Shreen Saroor takes up the serious challenges faced by Muslim women who have been dislocated by civil war, the 2004 tsunami, and the current revitalization of Islamic radicalism in east Sri Lanka. Her essay astutely details the specificity of Sri Lankan Muslim women's experience of the tsunami and with the subsequent NGO aid organizations that came in the aftermath of the tsunami. The proliferation of NGOs as a specific form of globalization that interacts dynamically with power relations on the ground has clearly transformed women's lives, gendered engagements, and social and religious institutions in the area. Saroor's and Silva's essays make clear that feminist scholars and activists must reckon with 'NGOization' as one of the most rapidly expanding manifestations of globalization. Their negotiations, Saroor demonstrates, have to negotiate legibility and survivability in relation to multiple sets of discourses.

The essays by Ananya Chatterjea, Piya Chatterjee, and Richa Nagar and Richa Singh push against the typical epistemologies of transnationalism; here, transnational feminism is as much about imagining possibilities as well as accounting for failures. In their diary of a social movement, Nagar and Singh recount not the easily identifiable and measurable outcomes of social organizing, but instead, the social and affective economies that sustain, drive, and impede such movements. In their vignettes, Nagar and Singh identify surges of insight, sacrifice, loss, and inspiration that illuminate the work of social movements, and the careful ongoing and incomplete dissolution of hierarchy, oppression, and privilege moleculized in the relations and interactions of the everyday. Chatterjea leaps off the page with her vision of transnational social justice through dance and corporeal movement. The praxis of transnational feminist transformation among a group of women of color enacts and engages multiple and shifting networks of power. Each woman stands in the node of her own history and world. Chatterjea details how Ananya Dance Theatre (ADT) allows each woman to account for and articulate each of these nodes and their attendant transnational connectivities. Slowly, ADT through workshop, rehearsal, and performance, disentangles and interlaces strand by strand a new network of transnational social justice. Piya Chatterjee opens another avenue into the exciting world of new ethnographic writing, an area that is gaining attention amongst cultural theorists. By focusing on the difficulties of scripting the histories and lived realities of women in the tea plantations of India, she elaborates on how transnational feminism and sisterhood solidarity can address the oppressive legacy of imperial power structures still evident in the disenfranchised population in the tea plantations, that is burdened on one side with complex, indecipherable linguistic codes and on the other side by ethical norms of ethnographic writing. New ethnographies move fluidly between and amongst different borders, and she acknowledges the tensions and anxieties of connecting ethically to the prevalent taxonomy that dominates lives in tea plantations.

Some of the questions raised here focus on the politics of advocacy and voice vis-á-vis feminist concerns, i.e. how is the marginalized subject presented and represented and whose interest are served in such representations? What forces propel global migrations and how do receiving states deal with 'unwanted' migrants from South Asia, especially in our post-9/11 reality? In turn, how do these migrants forge transnational connections through material and cultural process? What consequences arise from their imaginings via cultural productions and/or transnational advocacies? While such questions and their responses are often found in social science annals and policy journals, we wanted to emphasize the role the cultural processes play in these transnational connectivities.

Turning to social justice organizations, movements, and imaginings, what roles do global advocates and major financial donors from the global North invested in possibly improving the lives of women and children (like Save the Children and the Bill and Malinda Gates Foundation) play in crisis situations in South Asia? How do these organizations impact and interact with relations of power on the ground? How much agency is actually embodied in the actors who seek social justice? How do social movements on the ground negotiate, work with, or resist such organizations?

As massive global flows cross north, south and every which way, our abilities to navigate through and stand strongly in the critical nexuses, our abilities to reformulate and theorize transnational connectivities will shape the transformative politics of our present.

Acknowledgments

Gita Rajan thanks Gurudev and Rohin Rajan, and Jigna Desai thanks Khayaal, Rohan, and Ruskin for their invaluable support during this work.

Notes

1 See Amartya Sen's *Development as Freedom,* Knopf 1999, especially for a different, progressive implementation of development initiatives
2 See Chandra Mohanty's "Under Western Eyes" in *Feminist Genealogies, Colonial Legacies, Democratic Futures.* Eds. Alexander and Mohanty, Routledge, 1996; J.K. Gibson-Graham's *The End of Capitalism (As we Know It).* Blackwell, 1996; and Inderpal Grewal and Caren Kaplan's *Scattered Hegemonies: Postmodernity and Transnational Feminist Practices.* U of Minnesota, 1994.
3 See Valentine M. Moghadam's *Globalizing Women: Transnational Feminist Networks.* Johns Hopkins U, 2005.
4 Peggy Antrobus' *The Global Women's Movement: Origins, Issues, and Strategies.* Zed Books, 2004.
5 See for example, the following, Rosi Braidotti's *Nomadic Theory: The Portable Rosi Braidotti,* Columbia U, 2012 and *Transpositions: On Nomadic Ethics.* Polity, 2006; Amrita Basu's *Women's Movements in a Global Era: The Power of Local Feminisms.* Westview, 2010; Inderpal Grewal's *Transnational America: Feminisms, Diasporas, Neoliberalism.* Duke, 2005; Carol Gould's *Globalizing Democracy and Human Rights,* Cambridge U, 2004; Sandra Harding's *Sciences From Below: Feminisms, Postcoloniality, and Modernities.* Duke, 2008; and Vandana Shiva's *Earth Democracy: Justice, Sustainability, and Peace,* South End 2005, and *Staying Alive: Women, Ecology, and Development.* South End, 2010.
6 For more, see the edited collection by Myra Marx Ferree and Aili Mari Tripp's *Globalizing Feminism: Transnational Women's Activism, Organizing, and Human Rights.* New York UP, 2006.
7 Diane Detournay unpublished.
8 Quoted in Marx Ferree and Tripp, (82) and taken from Tripp's "The Politics of Women's Rights and Cultural Diversity in Uganda" in Maxine Molyneux and S Razavi's edited collection, *Gender Justice, Democracy, and Rights* 413-440. Oxford UP, 2002.
9 Clinton, then First Lady of the United States declared that women's rights are human rights at the Fourth World Conference on the Status of Women hosted in Beijing in 1995. This occasion also marked the 50th Anniversary of the founding of United Nations. This deliberate step in constitutionally forcing states to acknowledge women as equal citizens has had measureable gains in the fields of health, immunization, religious persecution, and economic empowerment. UN Women has adopted this claim in their mission, and has devised a set of rules for development dollars to be spent in keeping with a human rights angle and a gender-sensitive budget.

In search of the choreographies of daily life and struggle

Ananya Chatterjea

Department of Theater Arts and Dance, University of Minnesota, Minneapolis, USA

This essay is a reflection on the questions that have arisen during and consequently complicated the creative process as I have worked to infuse my choreographic work with social justice. Some questions have come from the troubling association of dance with entertainment only, ultimately broadening out to further questions about the function and possibilities of dance. Others have come from charges by activists that dance does not ultimately 'deliver' legislation that saves lives. Why dance then? In reflecting on these such questions I have sought to theorize my practice and parse out the ambiguities and contestations that necessarily complicate a practice that is intensely physical but also immediately metaphoric, and lasts only in the moment, in the labor of dancing bodies. Particularly important for me have been questions around dance and South Asian women's identities.

What does it mean to search for energy flow in your dancing while your activist friends are organizing protests and legislative action against female infanticide in South Asia, their journeys repeatedly interrupted? How to find joy in exploring complex rhythmic structures in a dance studio while you think about the tremendous effort and grit it took for Phoolwati, a young woman from Chattisgarh, to walk 110 km in five days, the closest point for her to access medical treatment for her burnt hands? How can I journey towards embodying a sensual articulation of feminine subjectivity in my dancing knowing that the brutal torture, gang-rape and murder of Manorama (July 2004), by Assam Rifles personnel in Manipur in the name of counter-insurgency operations, remains unacknowledged by the government?

Of course, patriarchal and state violence and lack of resources are neither the sole nor the definitive contexts for women in South Asia. Yet I struggle to articulate the spiritual and political valence of South Asian dance, different from mainstream forms such as ballet and jazz, as images from the Bollywood category of *So You Think You Can Dance* flash past – some classical mudras/hand gestures inserted in between virtuosic lifts and leaps, displaying 'perfect' bodies minimally fitted in 'exotic' costumes – and the ubiquitous presence of Bollywood threatens to overdetermine that 'Indian dance' is about dancing to fit into a hetero-normative notion of 'sexy.'

> Speak, your lips are free.
> Speak, it is your own tongue.
> Speak, it is your own body.
> Speak, your life is still yours.
>
> See how in the blacksmith's shop
> The flame burns wild, the iron glows red;

The locks open their jaws,
And every chain begins to break. (Faiz Ahmad Faiz)[1]

A revolutionary poet from Pakistan, Faiz transformed the typical form of the Urdu Ghazal, the love song, to exhort his readers to speak up against injustice and particularly against state violence. Exiled for many years of his life, Faiz was able to return only in 1982, but he died just two years later.

Dance your anger and your joys,
Dance the military guns to silence,
Dance oppression and injustice to death,
Dance my people. (Ken Saro-Wiwa)[2]

Saro-Wiwa was a Nigerian activist and leader of a non-violent campaign against the environmental degradation happening in the land and waters of Ogoniland as a result of aggressive industrial practices of the petroleum companies such as Shell. He died on 10 November 1995, hanged to death after a hijacked trial on unsubstantiated charges. In June 2009, 14 years after his execution, Royal Dutch Shell appeared in court to answer charges of crimes against humanity in connection with his death.

Saro-Wiwa and Faiz's exhortation to dance, even metaphorically, and speak, as resistance, are vital to my survival as an artist. These artists, along with many women artists and activists, who have inspired me in multiple ways along the way, many of whom will go unnamed, remind me that artistic work *can* be an integral force in the social change process. Yet, for me, it has been a long process to arrive at dancing as I do now, to find a way to dance that is embedded in the murky and gritty dailiness of our lives, as well as in the joys within the fabric of life; to dance in a way that is not immediately about entertainment, or a cosmetic beauty, or about some undefined notion of 'cultural transmission.' Indeed, it is after navigating many turbulent ideological storms that I have reached the understanding that my dancing can be a powerful articulation of the daily choreographies that structure our lives, choreographies of struggle, resistance, courage, and joy. The following pages are reflections on this trajectory, inflected by autobiographical details, but only to confer particularity to the conditions and questions that I believe many South Asian choreographers have to contend with.[3]

I have come to understand my work in choreography and dance as cultural activism, as a 'call to action.' Moreover, I work with an incredible group of women of color dancers at the intersection of artistic excellence, social justice, and community-building. However, when I began studying dance, early on, as a child in Kolkata, India, where on weekend mornings many girls went off to dance classes with a bag of ankle bells in their hand, I was content to dance for the fun of it. Gradually, the tension between the orderly world-view that dominated the classical repertoire, the joyful yet simple celebration of community in 'folk' dances, and the inequities of gender, class, sex, which were part of our lives but never part of these dances, became increasingly troubling. In particular, as an adolescent, I struggled with the contesting notions of femininity that were choreographed on my body, the strong goddess, or the shy petulant lover perhaps, from classical dance, the woman I aspired to become fitting into neither of these images.

Of course, beauty has its own power, especially when beauty is realized as a dancer finds a fleeting moment of perfect line, a moment that has behind it years of practice and dedication, but lasts only in the moment of its accomplishing. Virtuosity too can be a poignantly human endeavor, a continuous search for balance, only to have to find it anew every time. Yet, somehow through the glossed-over negotiations of post-colonial cultural maneuverings, in the need to establish a national identity through a celebration of a cultural 'heritage,' and as a celebration of the Indian government's motto 'Unity in Diversity,' dance in India, as elsewhere, has become largely commodified, part of a ruthlessly competitive touring and funding market, and more often than not, connected to ideas of entertainment, dance for its own sake. Clearly, this is a broad generalization, and choreographers like Chandralekha (1928–2006) and Manjusri Chaki-Sircar (1934–2000), who were instrumental in envisioning the category of contemporary choreography for Indian dance, strenuously worked against the grain of the market, creating strong feminist vocabularies and works.

> The only dream worth having ... is to dream that you will live while you're alive and die only when you're dead. (Arundhati Roy [6])

Gradually, moving away from classical dance performance, I began to experiment with forming a movement vocabulary that was feminist and contemporary. By that time, I was living in New York City pursuing graduate studies in Dance. Working in that cultural epicenter at that time forced me to chisel my politics as I continued my research in dance. First of all, while the rhetoric of 'muticulturalism' was everywhere, in the field of performance, it really seemed to mean that whites and 'others' could work with each other and engage in 'cultural exchange.' I seldom saw or found myself opportunities to explore encounters among multiple 'others,' particularly in ways that did not entail us being lumped into a group that emphasized similarity, however superficial. Second, how artists from global communities of color claim 'contemporariness,' especially in dance, is crucial to think through. Owing to the ways in which the global North has come to name and claim categories of innovation and radical artistic breakthroughs, whenever artists from 'other' contexts do create work outside of or extending 'tradition' (a space to which they are often relegated, or charged with preserving) or existent cultural practices, it is often assumed by broader publics that they are influenced or inspired by the 'West.'

> The East, in order to be 'contemporary' in its expression, need not have the burden of using the West as a crutch or ready reference. To me, to be 'contemporary' would mean to understand and express the East in its own terms. (Chandralekha 3)

While binarized signifiers like East–West are problematic and simplistic at this point in time, what Chandralekha is referring to and I am indicating, is the cultural dominance the global North continues to hold, and consequently the political, economic, and epistemological configurations it skews in its favor. Once again, the global North is not a uniform location, and within it are working class communities of color and immigrant and refugee communities who remain disenfranchised, while hierarchies of class, gender, and sexuality, for instance, conspire to create nexuses of power within the global South. Further, I mean to distance my argument about cultural specificity, about the particularity of material practices that make up the irreducible core of difference, from notions of cultural 'purity' or 'essence' and of cultural homogeneity. Fully acknowledging that cultural practices in any given geo-political space are usually hybrid, multiple, contesting, and constantly changing, I still believe it is urgent to argue for difference, particularly when it comes to constellations of specifically marked practices that characterize a genre, discipline, or style. The plié of ballet or modern dance is not a mandala, though the apparent shape of them might look similar. In the plié, the dancer bends knees and goes down, usually as preparation to come up into a jump or a reach, and generally supports the energy of these dance forms, which is one of aerialization. The arai-mandi of Bharatanatyam or the biparitamukha pada of Odissi, for instance, are basic positions the dancer inhabits: the dances are much more about groundedness, and the knee bend deepens that link and connects the whole foot to the floor, enabling fast footwork, for instance. In dance, these differences grow out of and in turn inform differences of aesthetic, in the values we attach to artistic practice, of notions of spectatorship, to name a few. This argument is particularly pressing now, as theories of a corporate-driven globalization flood public imaginaries, suggesting a utopia of equal and free exchange and global flow, but really ensuring and hardening existent hegemonies.

It was at the beginning of my time in New York, when I began crafting a movement aesthetic that was contemporary, based on a deconstruction of dance forms I had studied in Kolkata, that I realized it was important to clarify to audience members and funders, when they expressed that they appreciated how I had mixed my 'traditional' dance with movements from 'Modern Dance' (possibly because there was even less sense of contemporary South Asian dance), that in fact my dance had nothing to do with Modern Dance at all. Certainly, I have grown much more careful over the years, drawing my movement and pedagogical practices very specifically from deconstructions and extensions of the classical dance form Odissi, the martial art form Chhau, and yoga. Of course I had also studied folk dance forms in my youth so I am often influenced by those styles of movement. Arguments can no doubt be made that in working with folk dance elements I am repeating an appropriation from the working class and rural communities whose practices they originally were. Yet, in postcolonial India, fulfilling the Government's mission of 'unity in diversity,' many dancers learned a wide roster of 'folk dances,' adapted for the stage, presenting to varied audiences the diverse cultural life of the many communities and tribes in the different states of India. I did not know, then, to raise questions of 'authenticity' or 'appropriation,' and was happy to learn through these little cultural units about what I thought was 'the culture of my people.'

Moreover, the movement vocabulary I have created has also been shaped by the interpretations of my dancers, who often bring in idiosyncratic stylistic elements or elements from their training in Afro-Brazilian dance, or in t'ai chi perhaps, shifting the choreography ever so slightly. For me this hybridity is powerful, for I have often worried about the implications of working with a dance form based in Indian movement forms (the only forms I know well) while choreographing on the bodies of a diversely diasporic group of women. Excellence in dancing needs clear understanding of form and line and the aesthetic base of the form, and it is imperative for more reasons than one to avoid a vaguely sentimental multiculturalist collage of many forms of dance, in an attempt to be representative of all the dancers' 'cultural contexts.' Yet how can the dance form I am working with, emerging from a clear location in culturally specific forms, not become a huge colonizing gesture, where dance forms from India can articulate the stories of so many women from diverse communities? Making space for the deconstruction of forms, actively embracing and encouraging the hybridity, and sensing difference, so the dance is more often than not repetition with differences, has been important for us all to be able to dance together.

Moreover, often, because bodies are different, the movement sits differently on different bodies even as we dance the same phrase, creating a powerful statement about our difference and the power of dancing together, intimately, amidst that difference. One of the most powerful things I have learned to articulate as a choreographer is that ensemble work, which is crucial to my work, has nothing to do with sameness. It has to do with being rigorous about delineation of technique and ideas, but working with your own body to make that happen. In fact, while I deeply value our process which is as time and labor intensive as it is rigorous, I feel that it is in the way we are able to mark 'difference' clearly with our bodies as we journey with our audiences, from trauma through resistance to hope, that the greatest transformative potential of our work lies: difference within a base of solidarity. In addition, it signals a process of understanding movement, not through categories of ethno-national belonging, but as a site of knowledge production and creative labor, while marking political and cultural specificities.

The movement vocabulary is one way to articulate a politics of difference and particularity, the shape of the company is another. In 2003, convinced of the necessity of building alliances among women of color communities, I sent out a call to women of color who wanted to bring together dance and activism. This was a shift from my earlier efforts to build a company of South Asian dancers. Approximately 40 women attended the audition and 20 stayed on to become part of the project. These women trained together intensely under my guidance and performed in 2005, in the opening season of the company, *Bandh, Meditation on Dream*, which premiered at the Southern Theater. In the same year, a group of women who organically emerged as leaders lead a mission to institute the group as a formal dance company, and Ananya Dance Theatre was established as a non-profit in 2006.

Ananya Dance Theatre (ADT) is a dance company of women artists of color who are diverse in race, age, nationality, sexuality, but uniformly committed to the intersection of social justice and artistic excellence. Our mission is to create and stage original dance works and powerful images inspired by the lives and work of women all around the world, and to create different ways to understand and honor their struggles and resistance. Our dancing emphasizes the complex rhythms and power of footwork, the curvilinearity and sensuousness of torso movement (bakshya chalana) and the displaced hip (as in the tribhangi) of Odissi; the extension and spiraling of the spine, and breath work from yoga; the quick hip shifts and full-torso circles and side bends from Chhau. Movements from daily work from across Bengal, that I saw daily growing up or that are part of my daily repertoire of movement, are also part of my inspiration: hitching up the sari while running to catch the bus; picking through the rice grains and separating out the chaff on a kulo (woven basket); women walking through the busy streets of Kolkata with elbows out to the sides as I often did, protecting the intimate space of their bodies; the particular turn of the wrist with which women slapped on cow dung patties onto a wall, to be collected when dry to serve as fuel.

We believe that the search for excellence in artistry forges pathways to galvanize strong communities and generate forces of strength, beauty, and social justice. We believe that dance can be a powerful force for social change, presenting issues to our audiences in ways that touch the heart as well as the mind and motivate action. With every project we challenge ourselves in terms of artistry, execution, production values, and thematic content, and counter the widely held assumption that community-based projects lack artistic excellence.[4]

It is important to me and the women that I dance with that we understand the issues we work with from the complexity of our experiences immediately, and in terms of our corporeal and material existence. It is also important that the community we are deliberately forging through the process of working together is based on shared political goals, not essentialistic notions of identity. This means that we energetically resist reductive categorizations that might suggest that 'women of color' is just a constituency, and instead propose that this particular focus inaugurates specific theoretical, methodological, epistemological, and aesthetic imaginaries. This is how I understand the 'differential consciousness' that Latina activist-thinker Chela Sandoval talks about. This consciousness is vital as we discuss issues and workshop choreographic narratives, plan workshops, and respond to audience questions, for it posits, as Sandoval says, 'a tactical subjectivity with the capacity to recenter depending upon the kinds of oppression to be confronted' (Sandoval 59).

In ADT, we have also come to understand the difference between artistic work created on political subject matter, and work created through processes and driven by intentions and strategies of social justice work. This has implications for the structure of the company and the shaping of the creative process, the alliances we build in reaching new audiences and creating greater access to our work, and the activists we partner with in researching the issues and organizing around them. In fact, while my earlier choreographic work was still continuously focused on political themes, my work with ADT since 2005 has been focused on an examination of process, partnership-building, and year-round programming in order to implement an examined and thought-through model of social justice.

However, there have been difficult negotiations along the way. The impact of the work of cultural activists, like Kolkata-based playwright and director Badal Sircar or the Mumbai-based Stree Mukti Shanghatana (Women's Liberation Organization) Cultural Troupe, have assured us about the constancy of change that trickles through when we do our work. However, I have experienced a very real rift between the artistic world and the world of organizing in the US where I now live and work. This is certainly also true of the South Asian diasporic communities here. Social justice organizations often ask us for accountability in terms of measurable policy change, and often fail to recognize the work done by artists in terms of opening minds, creating empowerment, and generating leadership. Alternatively, there is a marked stigma in the arts field against artists who work with 'community issues,' and often a tacit understanding that social justice or community building work is done only by artists whose artistic talent is limited, whose work cannot stand on its own, and thus does not qualify as 'high art.' While inclusion in the realm of 'high art' is not our goal, we recognize that such notions often deepen the divide between both white artists and artists of color, and between artists working with Western mainstream dance forms such as ballet and modern dance, or artists working with 'classical' or 'court' forms, and artists who are working with alternative aesthetics. Our refusal to mainstream and our insistence on working along a relatively uncharted pathway in dance have caused us to encounter many frustrating road-blocks.

Of course, as performers, we do not leave behind a 'product' that can be used to measure our effectiveness. Nor do we work in ways that impact immediate policy change. However, we know that the bodily metaphors we create are significant in creating a different understanding of issues that activists and researchers often speak of in terms of numbers and logistics. This emotional access opens up spaces where healing and new encounters can happen, thus making possible processes of restorative justice. Of course, this means continuously organizing both within the company through movement workshops, information sessions, and constant dialogue, so dancers see themselves as agents of a social justice process, and outside with audiences, workshop and dialogue attendees. It means convincing those who journey with us as artists, activists, and audiences that performance can be effective as critique of mainstream policy-making, as a call to organize, as a way to build alliances; crucial, because we cannot accomplish a lot alone.

I am reminded of a story told to us by Richa Singh, an activist from the Sangtin Women's Collective, who participated in an exchange session with us. Richa shared the story of a little bird, which had her nest up in the high branches of a tree in a forest. One day a forest fire began raging and the bird realized that the life of her little babies up in the nest was in deep peril. The bird realized that there was no way to fly her babies to safety: as far as her eyes went, the fire had spread. Taking stock of the entire situation, the little bird flew to a nearby lake and began carrying as much water as she could hold in her beak and dropping it around her nest. The mighty fire roared with a laugh: You are a small bird; do you think you can dent my tremendous power with your efforts? The little bird replied: No, I cannot stop you, but at least I will not go down in history as someone who contributed to the destruction of life-force. Rather, I am part of forces of survival. This story has continued to inspire me and the dancers through time.

Through our process over the last few years we have learned that working collaboratively towards goals that are arrived at through community-based research and discussion can in turn create greater support for equitable means and solutions to address issues. Sharing space and building alliances, however, requires physical, intellectual, and emotional labor. Our work has required understanding that there are no typical models and that even though we have created clear strategies and processes, each collaboration and project necessitates that we build on our knowledge base and extend and deepen our work in new and innovative ways. The act of building community through artistic processes is often the work of building one relationship at a time, establishing trust over time, and there are no wholesale or fool-proof procedures.

Time and again, our workshops have repeatedly revealed the deep need to create more spaces where difficult dialogues among communities of color could happen, such that histories of alienation and hostility towards each other could be faced and the process of building new alliances begin. For instance, during an early circle discussion in 2004, an African American woman said that she had come to believe that, at critical times, she could only rely on her black and Latina sisters for support, and that Asian women would just 'go ahead and join the mainstream women's movement.' An Asian woman from Hong Kong responded that her experience was just the opposite: Asian women got 'left behind' because of their 'accents,' and other women of color just did not care about them.

For us, this was a foundational conversation: we recognize that both of these experiences are based in very real circumstances, and that there is a history of wounding in interactions amongst communities of color. Our job is to acknowledge this history and reverse its power by energizing healing and creating alternative realities. Working with our bodies in a shared space, articulating metaphoric images together, and participating in open discussion can reveal new channels of cooperation, while the repeated practice of laboring through anti-racism, anti-sexism, and anti-homophobic workshops together, can institute strategies of listening and of building solidarity.

In this way, my very different group of women, where no bodies look alike, perform a powerful rejoinder to the corporate model of globalization, where, in the name of bringing the world together, difference is often domesticated into superficial notions of diversity, like the United Colors of Benetton, like the availability of Coke everywhere, no matter that local industries have been devastated as a result of this 'global' uniformity. In this alternative response to globalism, where we recognize that we all arrive at this shared space through different histories, different experiencings of racialization, other questions arise: how to construct borders that must not be trespassed? How to re-conceptualize others so that we can engage in border-crossings that are transgressive, yet necessary?

In 2006 ADT made a three-year commitment to examining, through our artistic process, environmental destruction and its disastrous effects on global communities of color. When we began to work with community organizers to research the issues, what we had had in mind was that particular year's work, for the 2007 season. However, in the process we realized the immensity and complexity of the issues we were working with, and that we needed a sustained and steadily deepening study, creative process, and impact. This led to a trilogy of works, a piece premiering each year from 2007 to 2009, each piece exploring a different aspect of environmental justice.

The first piece, *Pipaashaa, extreme thirst* (2007), is a response to aggressive industrialization and toxic spills, resulting in bodily trauma and disorders, what our collaborators called the 'body burden.' We explored these through metaphors of madness,

Figure 1. *Pipaashaa, extreme thirst*, 2007. Photo courtesy of Ananya Dance Theatre.

images of acid rain and burning skin, where the struggles of people living in the arsenic triangle zone of Minneapolis echo those of communities in Abidjan sickened by the dangerous chemical waste dumped by a Dutch corporation. *Daak: Call to Action* (2008), the second project in the trilogy, focuses on land rights violations through aggressive industrialization and the consequent suffering of indigenous communities around the world, in the 'Special Economic Zones' in Nandigram and Singur, villages close to my home, to 'Free Trade Zones' in Tijuana and Suarez, and other cities along the US–Mexico border, and the appropriation of Native land here in Minnesota. *Daak* worked with images of home and homelessness, connection to the ground and lost connection.

Both these evening-length ensemble pieces concluded with images of women working together with breath to conjure hope. Throughout our process, we had felt that, despite the despair we felt at the immensity of the struggle still ahead, we needed to recall both for ourselves and our audiences the remarkable work happening in terms of organizing and resistance in small yet significant ways, very often the work of women, very often too the work of people from global communities of color, of people working with indigenous and equitable processes. Often, the best way we found to be able to translate this possibility of hope was by remembering that, despite lack of resources, and institutional and funding support, we were still dancing together and realizing this trilogy. The ending of *Pipaashaa* brought together influences from t'ai Chi, yoga, and the Manipuri dance form, heavily infused with breath work, where the dancers seemed to conjure down a rain of grass, like blessing, as they continued to dance. *Daak*, however, moved from exploring the blood spilled on the land, the destruction of the land and the communities who lived on it, landmines and factories, to a moment of thankfulness for the land underneath our feet, on which we were dancing. Entitled *Finding our feet*, this last section was lit only from the shin down, drawing a focus to the feet and the dance that was possible because of the ground on which we stepped.

Figure 2. *Daak*, 2008. Photo courtesy of Ananya Dance Theatre.

The last piece of the trilogy is *Ashesh Barsha, unending monsoon* (2009), an intense examination of issues of climate and energy justice. What we had begun to realize through the previous two projects reached full circle in *Ashesh Barsha*: that both the causes of these environmental disasters and the impediment to equitable problem-solving in addressing them could be traced back to hierarchies and conglomerations of power that ordered societies globally. We began to work with movement to explore questions of progress and 'efficient' movement, of blaming, rage, and the juxtaposition of excess (tsunamis and floods) and emptiness (thirst and barrenness). With this piece, however, we felt we could only end with a question. As the dancers strive to rebuild a sense of shared rhythm and community, they are disrupted through the appearance of manikins above them, who instigate a sense of competition among the dancers. Ultimately, the manikins disappear, and the dancers who have tried continuously to dancer faster and bigger through this sequence find themselves depleted of energy and isolated from each other. This fracturing of communities is in fact a very real consequence as resources dry up and marginalized communities are forced to compete against each other for their tiny share of these precious resources. The piece ends as the lights go out on the women who try their best to continue moving, and as three young girls walk out onto the stage, look at the women and at each other, and then finally look at the audience. *Ashesh Barsha* hit home in many ways, but mostly because it reminded us that energy is indeed finite and we need to use it judiciously. As dancers, this is one of our most previous resources, accessed through breath. As we liberally inhaled, our breath sustaining our dancing at a furious pace, we had to think of increasingly popular oxygen spas, where we were now paying to breathe in fresh air.

> In nature's economy the currency is not money, it is life. (Shiva 32)

The most obvious questions fuelling the trilogy are about how environmental issues, both in terms of causes and proposed solutions, are furthering racism and inequities between global North and South, and deepening hierarchies of gender and class in local

Figure 3. *Ashesh Barsha*, 2009. Photo courtesy of Ananya Dance Theatre.

contexts where state governments collude with multi-national corporations to sell our their people with no vision for the future. In addition, this long absorption in intersecting art-making and social justice work has continuously pushed further epistemological questions: how can women of color come to know the world in a way that empowers us to change it? How can we relate to global material inequities through the materiality of our own bodies? How can we work with our bodies, dance, breathe, to propel our imaginations so we can hint at a different way of doing things? How can we come to dance, know dance and enjoy it, in a way that it resituates us in the midst of life processes?

It is a difficult thing, being a dancer. I think it takes phenomenal courage and fortitude to agree to pursue excellence in a form in which the moment of doing is all you have. Dancing is powerful in that it can bring to life an empty space, fill it with vibrant color, breath, and rhythm, it can ensure connection with people who you share space with, those you are dancing with and those you are dancing for, bring incredible joy to your life, but you have to be a kind of Buddhist existentialist to endure. In the end, there is no material object left behind, possibly an injured body and no insurance to take care of it, much like the many activists who are organizing across the world now. Of course, there is memory.

I take heart in remembering that, by its very nature, dancing challenges the structures of capitalism. There is NO dance outside the dancers' bodies, there is nothing that can be extracted as a material object, no fruit of dancers' labor that can be bought and sold. There is only the bodily labor of dancing that produces meaning and significance in the doing, in the engagement, in the connection we can then create between you and me, and in the way we then learn to share space and rhythm. When I share space and agree that I will dance with fullness without running into my fellow artists, I learn a technique of collaboration as well, which can be vital for social justice work – different bodies, different ways of approaching movement, different ways of counting, dancing in the same space.

I also am encouraged by looking back at my choreographies and the collective artistic labor of a disparate group of dancers who come together in intensive labor, careful never to 'speak for' those who are not there, but to create abstract narratives that invoke the experiences of so many women, the particular circumstances of whose stories are different, but for whom the arc of injustice, trauma, and resistance is continuous. We are grateful to women across the world whose material practices of resistance and expressions of grief and loss have inspired so much of the work we do. It is from observing the choreographies of their lives – the getting up every morning to do the necessary work despite the disastrous circumstances that await them, to readiness to commit to life again – that has convinced me that the abstract dance of my choreographies can find a way to support the improvisational choreographies through which they navigate their lives.

Acknowledgements

For many updates on these ongoing struggles and efforts I am indebted to my friends across South Asia, who use several online tools as effective organizing tools. I am particularly thankful to Mumbai-based lawyer and activist Kamayani Bali Mahabal for her daily 'notes' and 'updates.'

Notes

1. This English translation of Faiz Ahmed Faiz's Urdu poem 'Bol, ki lafs azad hei teri . . . ' is by Azfar Hussain in *Reading About the World.*
2. Accessed 24 December 2009 from http://www.mosop.org/ – the website for the Movement for the Survival of the Ogoni People.
3. There is a deliberate oscillation on my part between locating myself in South Asia and in India. While politically I locate myself in South Asia, when I refer to specifics of dance it is important to site/cite my cultural context with accuracy in order to avoid the implication that Indian dance can stand in for dance across all of South Asia.
4. The move from 'I' to 'us' in speaking about my work indicates a methodological and political shift in my artistic trajectory, from working as a solo artist to working as part of a collective both in terms of the research and creative process and in terms of managing these projects.

References

Chandralekha. "Choreography in the Indian context." *Indian and World Arts and Crafts* Apr. 1991: 3. Print.

Hussain, Azfar. *Reading About the World.* Vol. 2. Ed. Paul Brians et al. New York: Harcourt Brace, 1999. Web.

Roy, Arundhati. *The Algebra of Infinite Justice.* Delhi: Penguin Books, 2001. Print.

Sandoval, Chela. *Methodology of the Oppressed.* Minneapolis: U of Minnesota P, 2000. Print.

Shiva, Vandana. *Earth Democracy: Justice, Sustainability, and Peace.* Boston: South End Press, 2005. Print.

Churnings of a movement: *Sangtin's* diary[1]

Richa Nagar[a] and Richa Singh[b]

[a]*Department of Gender, Women, and Sexuality Studies, University of Minnesota, Minneapolis, USA;* [b]*Sangtin Kisaan Mazdoor Sangathan, Sitapur, Uttar Pradesh, India*

This essay considers the relationships among silence, insight, violence, and possibilities in the context of movement making. It works through stories and vignettes associated with the lives of those who constitute a growing movement of peasants and laborers in the Sitapur District of Uttar Pradesh to explore the power of affect in shaping a political struggle. In so doing, the essay grapples with some difficult questions: what kinds of silences and sacrifices are borne out of struggles and how do they empower the relationships that make a movement? What violence may occur because of the political choices that a movement makes? Moreover, how does a movement find the hope and inspiration to grow in the face of non-stop violence?

Syracuse, April 6, 2007. For two women travelling from what some would call the third world of the third world, this is Surbala's and my eleventh day in the USA. Surbala, Richa [Nagar] and I were supposed to leave Syracuse University and reach Minneapolis today but we couldn't. The gathering that some of our supporters had planned in Minneapolis was cancelled. Northwest Airlines stopped twelve passengers from boarding the overbooked flight today, and the three of us were part of that group. And then began Richa Nagar's four-hour-long fight with the representatives of the Northwest Airlines – a fight in which Surbala and I could not participate verbally because we did not speak English. It was a fight in which no one screamed with anger but where an extremely tense argument with clenched jaws and hostile glances went on forever. I remembered many a dharna [sit-in]. This was also a dharna – a 'civilized' dharna in a land of so-called civilized people. The three of us remained solid in our collective protest. But I could not help thinking: 'What would have happened if only Surbala and I had been travelling today?' Everything that happened today broke my confidence to travel alone in the US. The long, hard journey from Sitapur to Minneapolis began to seem easier.... The humiliation that we lived today has sharpened my perspective.

In a world defined by casteism, I come from the category of discriminating castes; I have never been subjected to the humiliation that a dalit experiences, and even with my lower class background I have enjoyed the benefits of my caste-privilege without desiring them – sometimes in the form of an 'admiration' for my determination to fight and sometimes as compliments for my 'shrewdness' or 'cleverness.' I had known that race discrimination exists, but now I am seeing and feeling it. I am beginning to recognize the expressions of those eyes, which sometimes seem to be struggling to come out of their temptation to discriminate, and at others, seem trapped in the confidence of their assumed superiority. I keep realizing the ways in which Surbala's and my racial difference makes us weak here.... The ways in which it invites others to insult us.... It's not simply a matter of our color – it's the matter of our color that is intensely differentiated by its class, its language, its clothing, its walk, its smile.... This discrimination is more dangerous than caste discrimination because it begins with the eyes. It is not that the pain of caste discrimination is any less than this. But racial discrimination seems so quick and so dangerous – just like the automatic doors of this country – they open and shut with a speed that leaves us stunned. (From Richa Singh's US diary.)

Between late March and early May of 2007, Richa Singh and Surbala spent five weeks in the USA participating in a series of academic and activist forums in Minnesota, New York, and California that focused on discussions of Sangtin Writers' *Playing with Fire* and the movement building that emerged from our Hindi book, *Sangtin Yatra*. This trip was one of the hardest trips that either Richa Singh or Surbala had ever taken anywhere. It inflicted humiliations and silences that they had not encountered before. In addition, it produced tensions and tears among three *sangtins,* whose audiences, despite best intentions, could not escape the desire to judge who among us was the 'most authentic' *sangtin*. At the same time, the trip produced non-stop turbulences that led us to reflect, argue, analyze, and travel between our many 'heres' and 'theres' and it pushed us to work through our own stances and strategies to grapple with the shifting question of authenticity in ways that we found generative for the future of our alliance.[2] For us, this process triggered a search for new truths of the lives and relationships that have evolved since the writing of the *Sangtin Yatra* – lives and relationships that currently define the Sangtin Kisaan Mazdoor Sangathan.[3] This essay presents fragments of a few truths that owe their beginnings to this turbulence.

Humiliations, silences, and *roti*

Kailasha Amma of Khanpur does not know her age but to the outside eye she appears to be 60 or 65 years old. Like many members of the Sangathan,[4] Kailasha, too, encountered life's battles in such a way the distance between childhood and old age seemed to shrink into a few moments. No matter which meeting, rally, or *dharna*, Kailasha Amma is always there. But she is often quiet. Even when she is asked a question, she often stays quiet.

After the irrigation water arrived in the Sharada canal,[5] the *saathis*[6] of the Sangathan organized a movement-wide conference in Khanpur for two days. The preparations for this conference were proceeding in earnest. Donations were coming in from village after village. A few volunteers had just sat down to calculate how much cash and grain had been contributed when Kailasha Amma came up and, undoing a knot at the end of her *sari's pallu*, she pulled out a 50 rupee note and extended it: 'Here is my contribution!' Upon delivering the note, Kailasha returned quietly to the spot where she had been sitting.

Everyone was stunned. Kailasha, who has no flesh on her bones, has to struggle hard to manage even two *rotis* for herself at the end of the day. Sometimes the *saathis* hesitate to include her in the movement's work because her body tires easily. The conference became so important for that same Kailasha Amma that she gave away her whole day's earnings to this Sangathan. Kailasha's silent support spoke more loudly than the support of the most vocal *saathis*. Kailasha's refusal to seek recognition or to name her act translated her silent gesture into a sacrifice that inspired the *saathis*. Her sacrifice produced an affect through which the political meanings of a hungry body became inseparable from the power of the relationships that were emerging through the movement. This affect had the power to convert the rage generated by hunger into a profound hope of possibilities.

Kailasha's silent support continues today. More importantly, her silence reminds the *saathis* of a core question that is at the heart of the Sangathan's mission: how can the silences of *saathis* such as Kailasha transform the voice of the Sangathan so that the struggles, pains, and sacrifices of those silent *saathis* can register loudly in our collective direction, courage, and inspiration?

Languages of silence

When nine *sangtins*' pens started spilling ink onto paper for the first time, we chose to begin the journey by remembering our childhoods. At that time the *sangtins* felt intensely the shortness of those moments in their lives that storytellers and poets often remember as a phase full of colors, happiness, and radiance. However, as our journey progressed, we recognized the long, very long, presence of those childhoods in *sangtins*' lives. No matter how hard it is to recollect those childhoods and no matter how many tears the process of remembering triggers, the experiences of the brief childhoods lived on the margins continue to shape the struggles of adulthood. Our childhoods shape our whole lives: our speech, our silence, our confidence, and our anger – all remain entangled in the pasts of our childhoods. No wonder, then, that the reclaiming of the forgotten tongues of the childhoods suddenly instilled a new courage in the *sangtins* to ask why is it that one *saathi*, even after living one-third of her life becomes silent on those occasions when her heart wants to scream, and another *saathi*'s words overwhelm an entire discussion? As the journey of nine writers evolved into a journey of several thousand *sangtins*, the questions became more complex: why is it that one *saathi*'s childhood makes it impossible for her to speak without folding her hands before everyone and another *saathi* is convinced that the only way her own children can survive is by biting those who beat them? And how does the movement work to recognize both of these *saathis* as critical forces for the movement?

Of the many, many *saathis* who have worked to build the movement around the irrigation waters, and livelihoods, there are some who speak a lot, some who speak only at specific moments, and yet others who hardly ever speak. Whenever these *saathis* joined their silences in the voice of the Sangathan, we realized the extent to which the Sangathan's feet had been chained by their absences. On the one hand, thousands of our *saathis* strengthen their voices by associating with the Sangathan. On the other hand, it is only through the force of these *saathis*' voices and silences that the Sangathan learns the notes that it could never have recognized without them. The force of these silences and voices shifts the fundamental balance of who leads and who follows in the Sangathan and creates new possibilities for the future.

Manohar

There was a two-day training of *saathis* in Mishrikh. Most of the 50 *saathis* who came to participate had brought their own food for the first day. As the afternoon crept in, it became clear that some people had come without food. The lunch arrangements for these people were made. After lunch, Richa Singh was going to wash her hands and, seeing Manohar eating by the water tap, she sat down to chat with him.

> Manohar said: I could not arrange for the ration (food) for today.
> Richa: What will the children eat then?
> Manohar: There was some flour – they should be able to make a few *rotis*.
> Richa: And after that?
> Manohar: I will find some work. Otherwise, I will borrow.

Manohar, a member of the Maurya caste in the Azadnagar village, was responding to Richa's questions with a calm that suggested that none of this was a big deal. From his childhood, hunger has been an everyday reality for Manohar. Still, most of his waking hours are spent in the worry of how he will feed his children the next day. Was it this preoccupation that led him to stay quiet through most of the discussions in the Sangathan?

A few months later in May 2006 we suddenly heard the news that Manohar had sent away his daughter's *barat* (wedding procession) and the wedding was cancelled. This was disturbing news. While profoundly insulting to the family of the groom, the rejection of a *barat* also stigmatizes the bride and her family. Manohar is a widower so all the social consequences of this event in the form of gossip and lies would also have to be borne by Manohar alone. Even neighbors refuse to sympathize with parents such as Manohar at times like this because they fear that tomorrow their own daughters will remain unwed because of the badmouthing: *other villages will spit at us and say,* 'Barats *are sent away from their village. What's the point of finding a match there?*'

By the time Richa Singh made it to Azadnagar, the *barat* had departed. Manohar said to Richa,

> My daughter has no mother. I simply won't throw her away in a pit. First, it was the second marriage for the boy (groom), and second, they didn't bring anything that they promised for my daughter.... If they are mistreating her now, who knows what they will do later. I couldn't stand the insult and just turned the *barat* away.

Richa did not know how to reassure Manohar. However, the manner in which Manohar was stating all this suggested to Richa that he had stopped looking for sympathy or reassurance from others a long time ago. After going through the hardships that he had seen in his life, this new event did not come as a major surprise.

After this incident, Manohar started coming to the meetings of the Sangathan on a regular basis. But he maintained his silence. After several months, he shared with Surbala, Reena, and Richa: 'Earlier, I used to think that if I said anything wrong, you all will get upset.'

'Why? Have we ever been upset with you?'

What Manohar said in response began to peel off layer after layer of reasons behind his silence.

Manohar's childhood was spent as a laborer in the homes and fields of the *thakur* caste. At every turn, he heard the same rebuke: '*Abey*, mind your own business. Don't try to talk too much and don't act too smart.' When the children in the home of his *malik* (employer) played cricket, Manohar also felt like playing with them; but far from fulfilling this desire, if Manohar was caught even watching them play, the *malik*'s family yelled at him and did not give him *roti* that day. Through all his waking moments, a single message was hammered into his head – 'Know your place as a servant. There is no need to step out of your *auqat* [place].'

The bitter yelling and thrashings, day and night, burrowed into Manohar's heart and mind in such a way that even when someone asked him to speak, his tongue would stick to the roof of his mouth, and the snatching away of the *roti* that began in his childhood never stopped. This game of being kicked in the mouth and stomach since childhood is one that Manohar has learned to play well – almost like a machine. Without a tear, without a scream, without a noise.

Tama

It was on the day of our first *padyatra*[7] on the issue of irrigation waters that we met Tama in the village of Sabelia. Wrapped in grime and dust, Tama, whose eyes can see very little, was in his own world. After having walked for about 10 km and having held intense conversations in several villages, most of the *saathis* were getting tired. In such a mood of sweet exhaustion, one *padyatri* looked at Tama and said, '*Arey* Tama, why don't you sing a *bhajan* for us.' And Tama began instantly.

When someone asked, 'Who is he?' another voice answered, 'He is from this village. He is just a *Sirri*.' In Awadhi, *sirri* means crazy.

After this *padyatra*, Tama would appear wherever there was a meeting of the Sangathan and very soon every meeting of our Sangathan would get inaugurated with

Tama's songs. Gradually, Tama started singing the songs of the Sangathan and with a little bit of encouragement also started leading the chants of the movement with full force.

On 23 August 2006, it was with high hopes that the *saathis* planned a rally to protest the corruption associated with the newly launched National Rural Employment Guarantee Scheme (NREGS). This rally was at a critical turning point in the building of the campaign. The Sangathan wanted to build political pressure on the entire block and tehsil[8] on one key point – that its *saathis* should get their job-cards in hand without delay under the employment guarantee scheme. However, the rally coincided with a Hindu festival. As a result, a rally that was to begin at noon saw hardly a hundred *saathis* appearing by 11.30 am. Deep inside themselves, the organizers knew that rest of the *saathis* would show up; but what if they did not? The organizers felt stuck. If the rally did not begin on time nothing would happen at the tehsil office.

In such a state of doubt and indecision, all the *saathis* were standing in the *bagh* (garden) of Darogapurva. Across the street from the *bagh*, stood a little *thelia* (wooden cart) on which there was a megaphone. Suddenly, Tama moved quietly away from the crowd toward the *thelia*, grabbed the megaphone, and began loud chanting interwoven with one powerful song after another. His voice started raising the temperature of the crowd. As his resounding notes instilled a new excitement, the whole crowd became prepared to launch a *satyagraha* against its own humiliation and exploitation. The same Tama, who until now waited to follow someone else's lead in the Sangathan, was spreading such magic with his voice that the crowd was glued to him. On that day, the rally itself, a *gherao*[9] of the District Magistrate's car during the rally, and the rally's success in making the administration agree to its demands came off with such an unprecedented force that it begun a new chapter in the social history of Sitapur.

At that historical juncture, Tama gave the Sangathan the courage to build determination and hope in the face of growing hopelessness. Without delivering any speeches, he taught us effectively that assembling a crowd was not enough to build a powerful rally or struggle. In order to trigger energy, hope, and confidence in a movement, the people need a space to advance the movement's journey in their own way. The role that Tama played in the August 2006 rally raised him from a *sirri* to the category of the most active *saathis* of the movement.

Tama's emergence as an active *saathi* was not such a simple journey, however. Tama had not had opportunities in life that would have given him the tools to discuss certain issues with a strategic perspective. At times in the Sangathan's debates with the administration, Tama was so quick to speak in agreement with the development officers that the conversation would move in an opposite direction and other *saathis* became frustrated and angry with Tama at the challenges that his presence created. However, Tama's ability to speak his heart without fear or hesitation was the biggest source of strength for the Sangathan, and the *saathis* did not leave a stone unturned to create spaces in which this ability of Tama's could grow and guide the movement.

In January 2007, there was a two-day meeting of the Sangathan's active *saathis*. Along with many issues that were raised in that meeting, the idea of enacting a play on politics of wages and livelihood also came up. There were about 80 *saathis* present, all divided into four groups, each of which prepared a skit based on their experiences. It was the first time that many *saathis* got an opportunity to witness one another's hidden talents. The remarkable deftness and passion with which a number of them approached the art of acting took many by surprise. Of all those 80 or so *saathis*, it was only Tama who could not sit still after performing in one skit. Every time a group presented, he would arrive on the scene as a member of the audience to make one remark or another and, instead of leaving the scene, would just blend into each play and leave his imprint.

The group exercise made it clear to the active *saathis* that it was time for the Sangathan to prepare plays that would be ready to be used spontaneously when the opportunity arose in villages from where the *saathis* were emerging. To advance this idea, a group of *saathis* assembled in the Kunwarapur village and Tarun Kumar came from Mumbai to help us with this process. Tarun spent time with our *saathis*, grasping the nuances of their acting potential and then coauthored with Richa Nagar two plays, one on employment guarantee specifically, and the other on the politics of development more generally. This play authorship was challenging because those who were to perform the plays were not in a position to read or memorize a script. Instead, the plays had to be created in a way that the specificities of each performance could emerge from the everydayness with which our *saathis* live and learn the politics of livelihoods, development, and the employment guarantee scheme in their own lives. The task of presenting that living and pulsating knowledge in the plays required a fluid structure where the *saathis* could insert moments and lessons from their lives as the play was enacted. Tama became the inspiration for the performing *saathis*, who began to give their own twists, colors, and flavors to these plays in every new context.

As Tama performs in the villages, he sometimes navigates the play as a narrator and at others he becomes a laborer and represents the pain and struggle of thousands of laboring *saathis*. Whenever our *saathis* plan to organize a meeting on a burning issue in their villages, each one of them wishes that Tama could join their group. Tama's audience is enraptured by the manner in which he presents his ideas. As Tama talks, the audience flows with him. From where did Tama develop this matchless skill, this fearlessness, this magical poetry?

Born into a very poor family, Tama had not even begun to recognize life's colors when he started losing his vision. His parents managed to save a few rupees from their daily wages to devote to his treatment but, not seeing an improvement, they gave up. Tama does not even remember when he last saw the colors of this world. His mother just recalls one thing – that when Tama stopped seeing clearly as a little boy, he brightened his heart so that the external darkness could no longer affect his everyday life. Every day Tama battles with his grinding poverty. On the days when he does not get work, his family faces starvation. Unlike some of our other *saathis*, the possibility of going to a nearby town and looking for meager earnings every now and then is almost non-existent for Tama because of his blindness.

Many *saathis* are surprised by how Tama always manages to find an excuse to laugh in such adverse conditions. From where did he find this ocean of generosity, this warmth toward his cruel life? Is it possible that his laughter is his revenge against the absences and insults that life has thrown at him ... his way of taunting the world of the powerful and the prosperous in jest, as if to say: 'Keep hurling at me whatever pain and injustices you can. My *zindadili*[10] and I will not budge!'

The shrill critical notes hidden in Tama's *zindadili* and humor give an edge and sharpness to the Sangathan's voice. Once a meeting was to be held in Kutubnagar. The majority of the *saathis* got this news two days ahead of the meeting. However, Tama and a few others did not get the information until the last minute, so they did not come. When Richa Singh asked Tama why he could not make it, Tama said stubbornly,

> I could have come, of course, but chose not to; just so that you could learn how important it is to communicate such information to all the *saathis* on time. Would you have been able to come to a meeting if you got such late information? If the matter had been urgent, then I would

have made it with even less time in hand than this, but in this instance, there was a careless mistake. So I absented myself deliberately.

Richa apologized publicly to Tama for her oversight.

Tama sang *bhajans* in 2007. He sings them today. However, while his *bhajans* were devotional in the past, they now uncover the faces of those 'respectable' landlords, politicians, and officers who loot his land and labor, his dignity and *roti*. That is precisely why this bhajan of Tama's is now on the lips of every member of the movement –

Jab dil ki kuthariya saaph nahi tab Ganga nahaye se ka hoyi?
Panch banev, Pardhan banev, Sikretari kahaye se ka hoyi?
Jab photo ka paisa khaye gayech tab aphsar kahaye se ka hoyi?
Jab dil ki kuthariya saaph nahi tab Ganga nahaye se ka hoyi?

Karad bane, yojana bani, phiri talaiyya khodaye se ka hoyi?
Jab sabki majoori mari lehev, garantee lagaye se ka hoyi?
Jab janta duare ayi gayi tab danda halaye se ka hoyi?
Jab dil ki kuthariya saaph nahi tab Ganga nahaye se ka hoyi?

[When the storehouse of your heart is filthy, what's the point of taking a dip in the Ganga? What's the point of becoming a Panch or a Pradhan, or of being called a Secretary? When you ate the money for the (job-card) photos, what's the point of being called an 'officer'?

What's to come out of these job-cards, these schemes, and these commands to dig ponds? When the livelihoods are being stolen, what's the point of guaranteeing employment? When the protesting people have arrived at your gate, what's the point of swinging your baton?]

Silence and protest

Some children are constantly given opportunities to use their voices and some find themselves in circumstances where they gradually start identifying their own notes. However, there are many children whose voices are cruelly suffocated by society every time they try to express themselves. They learn to become silent – sometimes because of the schoolmaster's stick, sometimes by the slaps of the *malik*, sometimes by the thrashings from their Maa-Baap (parents), and often by the insults hurled at their own families by others. The little feet that start moving tentatively on the path of life begin to tremble at the very outset of the journey.

Those who feel most crushed by the dominant groups are frequently the same people who are dubbed *bevaqoof* (idiots) and *nalayaq* (useless) by the mainstream. These same definitions – like heavy *labadas* (cloaks) – become such unsheddable burdens for so many people in our villages that they do not get a chance to carve out new definitions for themselves.

As the *sangtins*' journey moved forward, the *saathis* began to understand the connections between these struggles – the ways in which the crushing of the voices from one's childhood and the inability to carve out the definitions to undertake an analysis of one's own conditions takes away the resources necessary for people to live a full life. Indeed, the very ground that is needed to use the opportunities and tools necessary to live a complete life are snatched from those people.

How deep are the relationships between the struggles of childhood, youth, and old age . . . and so tightly intertwined with our pasts, presents, and futures that one's childhood becomes synonymous with the history that is always present in one's struggles of today? Perhaps it is because of our childhoods' constant presence in our lives that the memories, desires, tears, and feelings dug from our childhoods have become a potent medium for building relationships in the Sangathan. Through the language of childhood, struggle travels from one soul to another, from one person to another, from one world to another.

When *saathis* of the Sangathan sit down to reflect on our childhoods, we quiver with rage. How does one begin to describe the childhoods of our *saathis* such as Manohar whose *roti*, at times, was snatched away for talking too much and, at others, for expressing a desire to play with the children of his *malik*'s family? Society thrashed him so hard that the waves that rose inside Manohar fell silent for years. He shut the doors of his heart and swore to himself that he would never open his mouth again. *Saathis* such as Manohar ask, 'the country became independent; the drums of democracy have been continuously beaten, but how do we break the chains that have bound us?'

Nevertheless, when Manohar found the space of the Sangathan his muffled voice started rising and blending with the voice of the Sangathan. Manohar says, 'When I sit in the meetings of the Sangathan, I feel that I have a place in this world. I feel valued. The fears that had locked my tongue for years are slipping behind.'

It is through voices such as Manohar's that the very intimate episodes and experiences of our lives find their grounds in the Sangathan. Somewhere or another in the intimate layers of all of our lives are experiences that we managed to recognize as injustice but were not able to create anything from that recognition. The merging of the silences and protests of *saathis*, such as Kailasha, Tama, and Manohar, with the voice of the Sangathan enables all the *saathis* to learn how to take the recognition of injustice to its next destination. Without the notes attained through this recognition the Sangathan could not have appreciated how deep a relationship exists between the following poem of Dhoomil, the suffocated voices of childhood, and the silences that have the power to break other silences: the struggle to reclaim *roti* is not simply about who rolls, eats, or plays with the *roti*, it is also about a silent violence of the powerful that can only be fought by enabling the silences of the deprived.

Ek aadmi roti belta hai.
Ek aadmi roti khata hai.
Ek teesra aadmi bhi hai.
Jo na roti belta hai.
Na roti khata hai.
Wo sirf roti se khelta hai.
Teesra aadmi kaun hai.
Mere desh ki sansad maun hai.

[A man rolls the roti/a man eats the roti/there is also a third man/who neither rolls nor eats the roti/he only plays with the roti/who is that third man? The parliament of my country does not respond.]

Murders, silences, and feminisms: Maya and Jinnati

Minneapolis, November 24, 2007. I have just hung up the phone after speaking with Richa Singh. Maya has been murdered. The same Maya whose fearless voice always drowned the voices of others, has herself been silenced forever. The corpse of the same Maya, whose forceful presence I associate with the beginning of our journey as sangtins, was thrown to rot on top on the garbage by her murderers – to mock all those struggles that Maya lived with her each breath, each laugh, and each scream and threw an open challenge to her whole society.

Her heavy sobs shaking with terror and anger still echo in my ears – 'All these people will kill me, just like they killed Jinnati.'

> And several of the women sitting around Maya in March 2002 had said almost in unison as they wiped the tears from Maya's eyes, 'How can they kill you, Maya. It isn't that easy to lose or take someone's life. Aren't we with you?'
>
> Five and a half years after that conversation, Maya was murdered in cold blood. Why? Because none of us could dare to live our most intimate relationships as Maya did? Because Maya did not allow any family, any husband, any job, any organization, or any ideology to govern her thoughts and life-style? Without ever uttering words such as 'NGOization' or 'feminism' from her mouth, Maya taught us most critical lessons that no one else could teach us – from her behavior, her relationships, her stubbornness and her decisions. Yet no organization, no movement, no companion could stop this fearless Maya from being murdered? Isn't this a major defeat for us all? (From Richa Nagar's diary.)

It was the year 2000. In the Arthapur village of Kutubnagar in Mishrikh Block, a man killed his wife, Jinnati, by stabbing her body with a knife multiple times. The whisperings suggested that Jinnati was involved in an extra-marital relationship with a young man from the village. Further investigations revealed that Jinnati was a second wife and her husband was many years older than she was. At the time of her death, Jinnati was the treasurer of the micro-credit scheme run in the Arthapur village by Mahila Samakhya-Sitapur. Outside a shop at a street intersection in Kutubnagar, one of Jinnati's friends said, 'What a tragedy that Jinnati's husband killed her so heartlessly.'

Hearing these words, a man from Arthapur immediately rolled up his sleeves and declared, 'What Jinnati's husband did was absolutely right. This is the best lesson for women such as Jinnati. If Jinnati were from my family, I would have gotten rid of her a long time ago.' Most people called Jinnati characterless and saw her murder as inevitable.

Anyone's murder, anywhere, is matter of profound pain and sadness. However, Jinnati was not just anyone – she was involved in so many discussions and debates in the Mahila Samakhya Program. No one doubted for a minute that she was emerging as a strong leader in her village. Yet, for those women who had plunged themselves into women's issues with Jinnati, her murder became a tough challenge. Far from expressing sadness or making efforts to bring her killer to justice, so many women from Jinnati's own village and adjoining villages busied themselves with trying to prove the validity of Jinnati's murder. Yet, these same women knew of several men from Kutubnagar whose extra-marital relationships were no secrets. At the time when people gathered to pay their last respects to Jinnati, it was not just the men who refused to show up. Even those women who were involved with Jinnati's own village-level micro-credit schemes did not step out of their homes.

The collective absence of women clarified the challenge that stood before the organizational workers who opposed Jinnati's murder: making any public comment about Jinnati's death meant inviting bitter reaction against all those women *saathis* who were becoming active on women's issues. The district level administration of Mahila Samakhya understood full well that women who publicly opposed Jinnati's murder would be communally blacklisted as 'characterless' women who 'want to turn all the daughters and daughters-in-law in the area into Jinnatis.' Even as hearts trembled with anger, they remained enveloped with the fear that no such word should slip out of any mouth that could become an excuse to push women back behind the closed doors of their homes.... At the same time, the organizational leadership recognized its responsibility: 'If we fail to question the society's definition of a good woman now, when would we take up this challenge? Isn't a silence over a foundational issue such as this one almost as big an injustice against Jinnati as her murder was?' In the end, the workers of Mahila Samakhya decided to organize a silent protest to raise this question in Sitapur.

In a tense environment, approximately 300 women from Kutubnagar marched in the silent protest against Jinnati's murder. At the main intersection of Kutubnagar, organizational workers invited the men from the area to join in. Approximately 100 men joined the *juloos* (procession) at that invitation, but left the march after covering barely half a kilometer. It was hard for us to tell how many of those men allowed themselves to open their hearts to the protest's message, but the *juloos* did bring an end to public discussions that had continuously proclaimed Jinnati as characterless. Later, Jinnati's husband was sentenced to life imprisonment.

How ironic that the cheerful and 'big-mouthed' Maya who remembered Jinnati's murder as she tearfully relayed the fear of her own end in March 2002 was brutally murdered within a matter of a few years. Actively involved in both Mahila Samakhya and SKMS, Maya was admired, feared, and resented for her wild and daring ways. Maya disappeared from her village, Narayanpur, on the evening of 21 November 2007, and two days later her corpse was found on the village's garbage dump.

The main cause behind the murders of both Jinnati and Maya was that they had intimate relationships with men outside wedlock. However, the quick pace at which Jinnati was accused of being immoral was something that did not repeat itself in Maya's case. In Jinnati's case, it also became a public fact that the perpetrator of her murder was her own husband, whereas in Maya's case it remains a mystery as to who her killer was. In the police networks, one did hear stories about Maya's 'illegitimate' relationships every now and then, but no concrete 'facts' were ever made public.

Together, Mahila Samakhya and SKMS organized a condolence meeting in Narayanpur on 26 November 2007. Besides prominent post-holding people such as Pradhanpati of Gramsabha Rannupur, more than 100 *saathis* from nearby villages gathered to pay their respects to Maya. All these people also participated in the six kilometer-long *padyatra* from Narayanpur to Kutubnagar that was held immediately after the gathering. The meeting and *padyatra* made it clear that no matter how many people taunted Maya for her *hekadi* (stubbornness), men from the Sangathan remember every gesture of Maya's with fondness and respect. For example, Shivram remembers how Maya often put her hand on his shoulder and said, 'Why Shivram, you say what we should do next?' Shivram's voice gets choked with tears as he remembers that *sahaj* (easy going) style of Maya. No matter how tired Maya might have been of the pangs of poverty, the chains of our society could not even touch her soul . . . her ways of embracing life. That is precisely why society could not tolerate Mayas's forceful laughter and honestly-lived relationships while she was alive.

However, despite this huge mistake of society, there was a powerful truth before us that made the tears shed after Maya's death very different from the suffocated screams that followed Jinnati's murder. When Jinnati was killed, the activists of Mahila Samakhya had to strategize how they could help people understand that the very attempt of justifying her murder was criminal, while also managing cleverly to protect those of its village-level volunteers who opposed Jinnati's murder so that no one could raise fingers and call them 'loose' or 'immoral.'

The scene in Narayanpur village on 27 November 2007 was intimately reminiscent of, yet in complete contrast with, what was seen in Arthapur eight years ago. Whereas not even one man had stepped up to publicly mourn the loss of Jinnati, several hundred men were present along with the Sangathan's women *saathis* to extend their respects to Maya. The manner in which people discussed the frightening meanings of Maya's murder as they remembered her was something that could never happen after Jinnati was killed. These differences forced the *saathis* to ask ourselves: even if a lot remains to be changed, what kind of transformation has already taken place that allowed our men *saathis* to cry publicly as they remembered Maya? What has changed as a result of our collective work so that our men *saathis* could angrily say that the accused should definitely be punished? Why was it that Ram Avtar and Bhainu did not try to lower their voices at the intersection in Kutubnagar as their tear-filled voices screamed with rage: 'An injustice like this against women cannot be tolerated! O, you killers, look at yourselves first!'

If Ram Avtar and Bhainu had not been *saathis* of the Sangathan, would they have been able to gather the courage to shame their community in this way? Perhaps not. Before we raise our hands to pat our own backs for this accomplishment, however, bigger questions scream at the *saathis* and make our hands numb. What is the price that the *saathis* must pay for this *mahaaz* (campaign) of social transformation that we have embraced? Has Maya been forced to pay that price with her own life? If this is true, why is it so? As these questions churn our hearts, we are also faced with the questions that our critics often pose before the Sangathan.

For example, one worry that has been expressed on several platforms has to do with the question of whether that the journey of nine women that began with the book *Sangtin Yatra* got sidetracked from its goals with the making of SKMS. Did the collective critique through which the *sangtins* had sharpened specific aspects of feminist thought lose its edge as the group transformed itself into an organization of laborers and peasants? This question acquires even more urgency in the context of Maya's murder. In departing from a sole focus on women's issues in Sitapur's villages and creating an organization of peasants and workers, has the Sangathan committed a strategic or ideological mistake that has resulted in our paying the price with the murder of a courageous companion such as Maya?

Whomever joined the journey of *sangtins* as a co-traveler saw at least one simple dream somewhere along the way: the dream of a society where someone who is poor does not have to be humiliated because that person is materially poor, is dalit, is landless ... or because s/he pulls a rickshaw or cart...; the dream of a society where memories of childhood do not inadvertently bring tears in the eyes of a woman or man ... where humiliations of childhood and difficulties of life, far from plunging the voices of our companions into silence, start echoing with the hope of bringing about a deep change.

In this simple and fundamental dream of living a life with respect, the *sangtins* could not see anything that should have been confined only to poor women. Nor did the *sangtins*, in connecting this dream with all the exploited workers and peasants of our villages, feel for a moment that we were leaving women behind. Are women not peasants? Are they not laborers? If the mere mention of a peasant or laborer evokes the image of a man's face in our minds, by what words should we define such feminist thought?

At the same time, a bitter truth has prominently informed the Sangathan's struggle: the everyday humiliation and tortures suffered by women transform themselves far too easily into murders of Mayas and Jinnatis. The everydayness of humiliation suffered by our men *saathis*, by contrast, does not place them at the risk of murder. The mockery of a woman's existence that happens in our homes and communities in the name of 'respect' and 'protection,' and the tireless efforts to crush her dreams and render her desires invisible are, after all, the everyday killings that become the stepping stones to gruesome murders of living, dreaming, and fighting women such as Jinnati and Maya. A fearless woman is battered inside her home so that she cannot advance her struggle with confidence and courage. A woman *saathi* returns home from a victorious rally on NREGS, only to be cursed in a public place by a husband or relative who wants to establish his/her power over the woman before the world – 'Look! She is under our control. No matter how strongly she might stand outside the home, deep inside we can crush her soul in whatever way we choose.' The Mayas who collide with multiple systems of domination are grave threats because the courage of their ideas and the force of their determination place in the circle of suspicion all their 'saviors' – from the district administration, the NGOs, the Pradhans, and the police to their husbands, lovers, and family members.

It is only by advancing these bitter truths in the Sangathan that we have learned the complexities of struggles that insist on identifying and finding their own notes in the midst of the terrifying possibility of being silenced forever. And it is these same truths that have enabled the *saathis* to see the violence inflicted by hunger as deeply connected with the violence inflicted by murder. If struggle against both forms of violence is intertwined and inevitable, then the Sangathan must also confront the risks and sacrifices that come with these necessary choices: for Kailasha that risk translates into giving up her day's food and for Maya it becomes the loss of her life. The difference in the magnitude of the two sacrifices shrinks with the recognition that both sacrifices are borne of a simple hope that the Sangathan enables – the hope for a dignified and fulfilling life. In a context where premature crushing of life is hardly news, *saathis* such as Kailasha and Maya pay the price of this hope with their bodies.

In lieu of a conclusion: 'No entry signal!'

After the rally of 23 August 2006, the gaze of political forces on the active *saathis* had become more vigilant. The same people who previously dismissed the *sangtins* as women working on women's issues, were now feeling threatened by the Sangathan's growing visibility. The economic equations that had emerged in the game of development were feeling the *sangtins*' burden. The information about when the *saathis* were planning which activities in which villages was now being assembled actively outside the Sangathan. In these circumstances, the three women who were working full-time as organizers – Richa (Singh), Surbala, and Reena – felt an urgent need to remain in continuous contact with the movement's membership. The long queues in the public call booths made it hard to discuss highly politicized and volatile matters with the members. Finally, Reena got a landline phone connection and Surbala got a mobile phone. Having access to the telephone made it far easier for them to do the planning associated with the Sangathan's activities. In the midst of all this, Sarvesh of Sabelia village said to Surbala one day:

'Didi, can you help me buy a phone, too?'

'Why don't you purchase some wheat to feed the family instead? The winter nights are cold and you don't even have a *razai* (quilt). Why don't you get a *razai* from your earnings? What will come from getting a phone?' Surbala lectured Sarvesh.

Then Sarvesh went to Richa Singh with the same request. Her response was similar: 'Sarvesh, I would not advise you to get a phone.'

Sarvesh went and purchased a telephone himself.

When Surbala saw Sarvesh with a telephone, she complained – 'Sarvesh, we tried to make you understand why you shouldn't waste money on a phone. But you didn't listen!' Sarvesh said,

> When you purchased a phone, did I ever try to tell you to not get one? That your expenses will increase because of the phone? Then why did you tell me not to get a phone? Isn't that what everyone else says? That 'when you poor folks get some money you lose sight of what your *real* need is. All you do is spend your money on wasteful things such as radios and phones.' When you told me the same thing, I was incensed. So I just went and purchased a phone.

When Surbala first heard Sarvesh's words, she was livid, but soon her anger turned into an intense restlessness. Why did Sarvesh interpret her advice in this way? After several days, Surbala discussed this issue in a meeting with other *saathis* and confronted the truth of what Sarvesh said. Can she or Richa or any other *saathi* truly assess what Sarvesh can or cannot do with the wages of his sweat? Can they determine what is or is not his need? Is it not true that despite their best intentions, those who organize and 'lead' movements end up pointing their fingers at Sarvesh's *tabqa* (class) and their ideas about his *tabqa* lead many to presume and define things for that *tabqa*? Why? Just because they have tried to stand with them or extended a little bit of support in their fight for their *roti*? Sarvesh's *tabqa* is the one that supports our movements precisely like a thumb blends with our hand to reinforce it into a powerful fist; and even after reinforcing the fist it never preaches at anyone. Then why is it that Surbala assumed that she knew what Sarvesh's need was?

Today, Surbala does not mind Sarvesh's purchasing of the phone or his harsh directness with her. In fact, somewhere or the other she sees these as 'no-entry' signals: no-entry signals that remind Surbala that she has no right or ability to decide how Sarvesh's life should carry on, what his needs are, or what would give him happiness. Remembering this incident, Surbala wrote in her diary,

> After this incident, my relationship with Sarvesh has grown deeper. Now when the people of our villages return with a radio in their hands after pulling the cycle rickshaws in Lucknow, I do not flinch. I still wrestle with the questions – 'Why did they purchase this radio? Wasn't their need something else?' But I don't dare to think that I am even in a position to understand the answers.

Sarvesh, like Tama and Manohar, pushes us to confront the reality that the Sangathan's collective struggle for recognition of injustice is impossible without a recognition of the limits imposed by each *saathi's* own privileges and perspectives ... our own inability to fully know any *saathi*'s feelings, desires, actions, or reasoning. It is this politics of recognition that gives all the *saathis* of the Sangathan the tools to measure the sacrifices of Kailasha and Maya, and to derive courage and inspiration from them.

Acknowledgements

Jigna Desai's brilliant and insightful comments and Marion Werner's thoughtful questions on a previous version of this essay helped us to weave together these translated excerpts in their present form. The authors acknowledge our debt to David Faust for his faith in this work and his willingness to read, comment, and challenge countless times.

Notes

1. This article has been developed from excerpts of forthcoming book in Hindustani, *Sangtin Yatra Jari Hai*. *Sangtin Yatra Jari Hai* embraces some of the key intellectual and political challenges articulated in *Sangtin Yatra/Playing with Fire*, and presents an analysis of the processes by which the public debates generated by *Sangtin Yatra/Playing with Fire* translated into the making of Sangtin Kisaan Mazdoor Sangathan (SKMS), a movement of 5000 peasants and laborers, and how this movement has tried to provide an ongoing critique of mainstream projects of empowerment while also pushing the state to implement its own policies adopted in the name of 'the poor.'
2. The questions pertaining to authenticity that arose in the context of discussions in the US played out very differently than they had done in *sangtins'* alliance work in India, and the political meanings embedded in these dialogues were also quite different. While a detailed discussion of this topic is outside the scope of this article, we would like to share a broad point: the intensity of

our emotional engagement with how each of us was read and interpreted as part of SKMS and our gradual 'discovery' that our responses emanated from the audiences' desire to 'know' the 'true *sangtin*,' led us to locate this desire *and* our responses in relation to (a) the complex processes pertaining to the making/representation/translation of a movement such as SKMS; and (b) the cultural and political economies through which 'knowledges' about the Other are produced, processed, consumed, and made into objects (of study, charity, admiration, and/or pity) in the global academic and non-profit industrial complex.

3. Sangtin Kisaan Mazdoor Sangathan (SKMS) is an organization of peasants and workers working in Mishrikh and Pisawan development blocks of Sitapur District in the Indian state of Uttar Pradesh. More than half of SKMS's members are women and over 95% are dalit. The three full-time organizers (Richa Singh, Surbala Vaish and Reena Pande), who were working to build the movement in the villages of Sitapur in 2005–2006, are from the *sawarn* castes.
4. The term *Sangathan* throughout this chapter refers to the movement led by the organization, SKMS.
5. In 2005–2006, more than two thousand members of SKMS mobilized to return the flow of irrigation waters to the Islamnagar distributary channel of the Sharada Canal. This channel was dry and had been written off as unusable, even though the Uttar Pradesh Irrigation Department continued to issue contracts for its cleanup every year. After several months of organizing in over 60 affected villages and sustained non-violent campaigning at the block and district offices of the Irrigation Department, water was released into the canal in 2005 for the first time in 16 years. The water has continued to flow through the canal since then.
6. *Saathi* means friend or companion and refers to a member of the movement.
7. *Padyatra* refers to a long march, in this case from village to village, to mobilize people on a particular issue.
8. A *block* refers to a 'rural development block' and a *tehsil* is an administrative unit of governance.
9. *Gherao* can be described as a protest where people surround or detain a person in power.
10. *Zindadili* is derived from *zinda dil*, or a heart that is alive. The term denotes a passion for life.

Citizenship and dissent: South Asian Muslim youth in the US after 9/11

Sunaina Maira

Asian American Studies, University of California, Davis, USA

This essay focuses on issues of dissent and citizenship for South Asian Muslim immigrant youth after 9/11 as they intersect with questions of youth culture and cultural consumption and are inflected by class and gender. Everyday experiences of national belonging or cultural citizenship for these youth are shaped by US imperial power, and what I call 'imperial feelings,' and by the biopolitics of neoliberal capitalism. Based on ethnographic research on a group of working class South Asian immigrants in a US high school, the article explores the expressions of dissenting citizenship of these immigrant youth and their responses to the War on Terror. It discusses the ways in which dissenting citizenship is linked to issues of cultural consumption, cyberculture, and notions of neoliberal citizenship, on the one hand, and the proliferation of gendered notions of dissent and 'good' Muslim identity that are marketed and consumed, on the other.

Introduction

This essay examines the ways in which South Asian youth in the Diaspora engage with notions of citizenship in relation to disciplinary regimes of the global War on Terror and neoliberal capitalism. It focuses on South Asian immigrant youth in the US after 9/11, exploring youth culture as a key site of contestation and negotiation of nationalisms, gender, sexuality, racialization, labor, and the US state. In general, youth are the locus of deep anxieties about local, national, and global processes and their impact on the nation, for they are assumed to embody the future and the possibility of change or continuity; these anxieties are exacerbated in the case of immigrant youth, and in particular Muslim youth in the post-9/11 moment.

The construction of youth as a 'transitional' category of citizenship underlies the preoccupation with youth in relation to the social order and civic personhood. However, youth are often neglected in work on historical processes of nationalism and globalization, because they are viewed as less important social actors. There is often an under-theorization of young people's actual social, material, and political concerns in relation to the major debates across disciplines, such as about nationalisms and globalization. I have tried to offer an intervention in the field of youth and cultural studies, drawing on Arjun Appadurai's framework for globalization, by developing an epistemological and methodological approach, 'youthscapes,' that links popular culture practices, national ideologies, and global markets and migrations (Maira and Soep 15–35). This inter-disciplinary model for youth culture studies integrates an analysis of expressive cultural forms produced by youth with materialist and historicist approaches, countering the tendency by some scholars in the US to focus on cultural production and consumption by youth, or questions of identity and representation, divorced from larger political contexts.

This essay discusses an instance of a youthscape, focused on Muslim immigrant youth from India, Pakistan, and Bangladesh living in the US after 9/11 and their experiences of citizenship and national belonging in everyday life. The study explores the ways in which these young immigrants responded to the War on Terror, waged both within and beyond the borders of the US, and imagined their national, ethnic, and religious identities in relation to cultural forms – including but not limited to media – in local, national, and transnational contexts. The article draws on an ethnographic study I did from 2001–2003, that examined how issues of national belonging play out in the spheres of education, popular culture, and labor for young immigrants, linking citizenship to work, consumption, subcultural affiliation, cross-ethnic solidarity, and (trans)national belonging for South Asian Muslim youth. These questions have been underexplored in existing work on Muslim American youth, which has tended to have a rather narrow and sometimes Orientalist focus on issues of gender and Islam, cultural clash and inter-generational conflict, neglecting issues of class, popular culture, and political subjectivity. The larger project (Maira *Missing*) challenges the dominant fictions about Muslim immigrant youth and the desire to 'know' them as a distinct, and potentially suspect, 'other.' The study considers its subjects to be much more than just 'Muslim youth,' portraying them also as immigrants, students, workers, family members, and cultural consumers. It has three major focal points – youth, citizenship, empire – and it questions the relationship among and between these pivotal concepts in order to offer a deeper, more critical understanding of what has been glossed as the 'post-9/11 moment.'

My research focuses on a group of working to lower-middle class South Asian immigrant youth living in a New England city I call 'Wellford' and grappling with issues that extended well before and after the events of September 11. However, in the wake of the 9/11 attacks, questions of citizenship, racialization, religion, and national identification took on new, urgent meanings for South Asian Muslims living in the US and Muslim and Arab Americans more generally, as well as South Asians mistakenly profiled in the post-9/11 backlash, particularly (turbaned, male) Sikh Americans, and other 'Muslim-looking' or 'Middle Eastern-looking' people. The national allegiances of Muslim, Arab, and South Asian Americans came under intense scrutiny for signs of betrayal to the project of 'freedom' and 'democracy' as defined by the state in its global War on Terror. This 'youthscape' connects the experiences of young immigrants to issues of state policy, domestic and foreign. It examines the impact of the imperial state on the everyday lives of young people from communities targeted as suspect citizens or aliens outside the nation as part of a civilizational discourse about modernity, violence, and democracy.

The study: Cultural citizenship and imperial feelings

The South Asian immigrant youth in my study were predominantly working- to lower-middle class, with minimal to moderate fluency in English, and belonged to the most recent wave of immigration from South Asia to the US. The majority of the Indian immigrant high school students were from Muslim families, most from small towns or villages in Gujarat in western India. Most of the South Asian youth had migrated within the last seven to ten years, though some had fathers or relatives who had come to the US on their own much earlier. Several of the South Asian Muslim youth were actually related to one another as their families were part of an ongoing chain migration. Their parents generally worked in low-income jobs in the service sector, and they themselves worked after school, up to 30 hours a week, in fast food restaurants, gas stations, retail stores, and as security guards. However, their urban, working-class experiences were often completely unknown to their more privileged South Asian counterparts in the area.

The experiences of these youth are shaped by the local context of Wellford, a small, predominantly white city that was transformed in the 1990s by accelerated gentrification and by increasing immigration.[1] The Wellford public high school has an extremely diverse student body, including immigrants from Latin America, the Caribbean, Africa, and Asia.[2] Reflecting more or less the national immigration trends for South Asians in the US, the largest South Asian group in the high school was from India, followed by Pakistan, Bangladesh, Nepal, Tibet, and Afghanistan. Students from South Asia constituted the largest Muslim population in the school, followed by youth from Ethiopia, Somalia, and Morocco.[3] During this time, I was a volunteer with the South Asian Mentoring and Tutoring Association (SAMTA), a program that helped to organize workshops for South Asian immigrant students on academic, cultural, and political issues. The research is informed by a range of connections as well as dis-connections I experienced with these young people, including issues of cultural familiarity, generational and religious differences, and class fissures that exist in the larger community as well.

The larger project explores various ways in which South Asian Muslim youth understood everyday experiences of inclusion or exclusion, or cultural citizenship (Ong 737–762). After 9/11, but also at other moments in US history, cultural definitions of citizenship and dominant understandings of who is truly 'American' mediate the rights afforded to citizens and immigrants and cultural constructs of 'terrorists' (now 'jihadists'), 'borders,' and 'security.' Muslim youth, particularly young males, are inextricably associated with the specter of radical Islam and fundamentalist militancy via an explicit, or sometimes implicit, Orientalism and Islamophobia exacerbated by anti-Arab racism. Muslim females are seen as inherently oppressed by their religion, and cultural traditions, and in need of rescue by 'the West' (Razack). The notion of cultural citizenship highlights the ways in which the trope of national belonging, so powerful in modernity, is based not just on the political and economic dimensions of citizenship but is also defined in the cultural realm of belonging. These questions are especially pertinent to youth, who are viewed as the next generation of 'citizens' and are often focal points in debates about national culture (France 200). At the same time, cultural belonging is still intertwined with legal distinctions between citizens and non-citizens and issues of immigrant rights and worker rights. My research demonstrates how issues of national belonging play out in the spheres of education, popular culture, and labor for young immigrants, linking cultural citizenship to work, consumption, subcultural affiliation, cross-ethnic solidarity, and (trans)national belonging for South Asian Muslim youth.

Citizenship is not just embedded in, but actually constitutive of, the workings of empire and the management, as well as resistance, of its subjects. The possibilities and limitations of citizen rights have been shaped by the evolving form of the nation-state, the administrative practices of colonial (and postcolonial) regimes, the demands of the market, and emerging supranational governmental institutions (Hindess 241–256). My research builds on the historical analysis of the cultures of US imperialism by Amy Kaplan and Donald Pease to look at the lived experience of empire within the nation. The study connects the experiences of Muslim immigrant youth to the 'imperial feeling' of post-9/11 America, the complex of psychological and political belonging to empire that is often unspoken, but always present. I argue that imperial feelings undergird what William Appleman Williams called 'empire as a way of life,' or the 'habits of heart and mind' that infuse and accompany structures of difference and domination (Stoler 2). Imperial power maintains dominance outside the nation through the 'policing of domestic racial tensions' and disciplining of subordinated populations through gender and class hierarchies at home (Pease 31; Román 269–284).

In putting US empire at the center of the story, I have shifted the frame from worn dichotomies of assimilation/ethnicization and a nation-based focus on immigration, or a narrow focus on religion and cultural difference, to an analysis linking the domestic and global faces of imperial policies. While the term 'empire' has recently become (re)attached to the US in ways that are normalized, and even fashionable, it suggests divergent analyses and political critique. US imperialism is marked by invisibility, secrecy, and flexibility in its operation of power, and by nebulous, non-territorial forms of domination that do not resemble traditional forms of territorial 'colonialism,' which facilitates the collective amnesia or denial of US empire. In this project, I emphasize that the post-9/11 moment is not exceptional, but part of a longer history of US imperialism and political repression that has generally been evaded or erased. The 'post-9/11' moment is not a radical historical or political rupture, but rather a moment of renewed contestation of the state's imperial power and ongoing issues of war and repression, citizenship and nationalism, civil rights and immigrant rights.

The 'state of emergency' after 9/11 – this crisis of civil rights and the dissent it provokes – is not exceptional in the US, even if it becomes more apparent at certain historical moments and for certain groups (Ganguly). The theory of the 'state of exception' suggests that the expansion of executive power and suspension of democratic rights is, in fact, not the exception but the rule – the constitutive paradigm of Western government and law since World War I – blurring the distinction between 'peace and war' (Agamben 22). As Michael Hardt and Antonio Negri (17) point out, the state of exception is permanent for empire which, as a rule, exercises repressive, preventive, and military force. The post-9/11 moment builds on measures and forms of power already in place – this is a state of everyday life in empire.

One of the aims of this research is to reflect on what it means to express political views dissenting from the majority when the freedom to critique the state is particularly tenuous for certain groups, based on national origin and religion. In this study, I chose to focus on a group of young people who would not conventionally be defined as political 'activists' and who did not belong to any organized political groups or even community organizations. The analysis of these young people's political critique goes beyond the question of political rights and organized activism to the many contexts in which political subjectivity are produced and to the meaning of the 'political' itself.

Dissenting citizenship

In this article, I am going to focus on a particular form of cultural citizenship expressed and performed by South Asian Muslim youth in the post-9/11 moment, what I call dissenting citizenship. I will touch on ways in which dissenting citizenship is linked to issues of cultural consumption and notions of neoliberal citizenship, on the one hand, and the proliferation of gendered notions of dissent and Muslim identity that are marketed and consumed, on the other hand.

As the state acquired sweeping powers of surveillance with the PATRIOT Act, there were numerous incidents of FBI and police investigations of 'un-patriotic' statements or activity that have been variously frightening and absurd (Rothschild). In the face of such repression, I found these South Asian Muslim immigrant youth to be engaged in a practice of dissenting citizenship: an engagement with the nation-state that is based on a critique of its power and rhetoric, and not automatically or always in compliance with state policies. The youth in my study did not use a formal political vocabulary of state and empire, but they still offered critiques of racism, Islamophobia, war, and foreign policy and grappled with an ethics of belonging. Criticism of the state's rationale for the collective punishment of Muslims and the US War on Terror was pervasive. For example, Ayesha, a girl whose family was from Gujarat in western India, observed, 'Just because one Muslim did it in New York, you can't involve everybody in there, you know what I'm sayin'.' A week after 9/11, Ayesha chose to write the words 'INDIA + MUSLIM' on her backpack. For her, this was a conscious gesture of defiance, for she knew well the possibility of repercussions for those publicly identified as Muslim, but was not afraid of backlash. She said staunchly, 'I'm hard-headed, that's how I am.' Other youth emphasized the importance of political justice and respect for international human rights, denouncing both the terrorist attacks and militarized state aggression as a means of retribution. Zeenat, a newly arrived immigrant from Gujarat, commented on the US war on Afghanistan in response to the attacks by Al Qaeda, 'I think it's wrong, they didn't attack the United States, they didn't bomb on this country, right? So why we are bombing on their country?'

All of these youth challenged the state's rhetoric about the 'liberation' of Afghanistan and the 'collateral' killings of civilians, critiquing what was understood by many in the US to be a 'just war' in terms of human rights and international justice and linking it to nationalisms and state-sponsored terror. Jamila, a Bangladeshi girl, was one of several students who spoke of the need for the US government to provide 'proof' of who was really culpable in the 9/11 attacks and who condemned the killing of 'innocent people who had nothing to do with it,' holding the state accountable for offering its citizens evidence to justify its War on Terror. The dissent of these Muslim immigrant youth was clearly driven by two factors: they had been forced to deal with state and civil society discrimination targeting their communities soon after arriving in the US, and they were from a region that was experiencing a US military invasion at the time (in Afghanistan). Their persistent, if not strengthened, identification as Muslim seemed to be partly a defiant response to Islamophobia, scapegoating, and collective punishment targeting Muslims, Arabs, and 'Muslim-looking' people.

However, the notion of dissenting citizenship that I propose is not meant to suggest that dissent by South Asian Muslim immigrant youth, or South Asian or Muslim Americans more generally, was overt or consistent, let alone that it is inherently guaranteed. Not all the students were as bold as Ayesha in challenging the profiling of Muslims and publicly claiming a Muslim identity – which Ayesha did without wearing a hijab, contrary to expectations of what religious identification looks like for Muslim girls. After 9/11, South Asians, Arabs, and Muslims across the US were increasingly hesitant to speak publicly about political issues. As Corey Robin (199) points out, repression historically works on two levels to silence dissent: on a state level, but also on the level of civil society, where individuals internalize repression and censor themselves. Practices of racial profiling and detention that have long targeted other groups, such as African Americans and Latinos, not to mention the brutal subjugation of Native Americans, similarly represent 'political technologies of the body' whose disciplining effects are not restricted to those bodies actually detained within prison walls, but (not unintentionally) extend to others who internalize these disciplinary regimes (Hansen and Steputat 12).

Furthermore, dissenting citizenship is still a form of citizenship, and engages with the role and responsibility of the nation-state and the question of belonging and rights for subjects, however marginalized, so it encapsulates the contradictions of challenging the state while seeking inclusion within it. As 'transmigrants,' or migrants with transnational ties (Basch, Glick Schiller, and Blanc), these young immigrants strategically use citizenship and the framework of immigrant and citizen rights, trying to advance from one category of protection and entitlement to the other. Dissenting citizenship captures some of the ambivalence toward the US that these youth experience, for it is simultaneously a place invested with their parents' desire for economic advancement and their own hopes to belong in a new home, and also the site of alienation, discrimination, fear, frustration, and outrage. A few young immigrants had expectations that the US would live up to its mythologized deals of freedom and equal rights, but most seemed to emphasize simply that US actions should be held to an international standard of justice that should apply to all nation-states, including their home countries of India and Pakistan.

Interestingly, for these Muslim immigrant youth after 9/11, the high school was one of the few, if only, public spaces where they felt comfortable discussing politics, mainly because of the support of progressive teachers and staff. The public school, in both formal classes and informal conversations between teachers, staff, and students, inculcated ideals of civic engagement and liberal democratic notions of racial justice and minority civil rights. For example, after an anti-Muslim incident in the high school involving Adil and Walid, two Pakistani boys, the school organized an assembly featuring two Arab American speakers who criticized the war on terrorism and the attack on civil liberties. Adil, Walid, and an Indian Muslim girl, Shireen, delivered eloquent speeches condemning racism to an auditorium filled with their peers. Adil said that when he was threatened by some young men in the city, 'I could have done the same thing, but I don't think it's the right thing to do.' Adil was a muscular young man and his call for non-violent response was a powerful one at that assembly, especially at a moment when the US was bombing Afghanistan in retribution for the attacks of September 11, and it implicitly spoke to the larger question of violence, war, and international human rights. Shireen appeared on stage in her salwar kameez and said, 'We have to respect each other if we want to change society. You have to stand up for your rights.' Even though these working-class immigrant youth did not have the time to participate in organized activism, they seemed to have become spokespersons in the public sphere engaging with the discourse of 'rights' and with civil and immigrant rights debates in the local community.

The process of dissenting citizenship is not without important tensions that animate its expression, for I found these young immigrants implicitly understood the limits of a state-based notion of citizenship, in its economic, cultural, and political senses, and the limits of 'rights' afforded by the state. Muslim immigrants from India, in particular, have had to consider the failures of both home and host states – India and the US – to guarantee protection and equal rights to Muslim subjects. The anti-Muslim massacres in Gujarat in spring 2002, as well as other attacks by right-wing Hindu movements in India, and the military standoff between India and Pakistan that preceded it, reinforce for Indian Muslim youth their ambiguous location between religious and national identification, for their national allegiances are questioned in India as part of a larger discourse about 'Islamic terrorism' and a fifth column that echoes fear-mongering in the US.

Right-wing Hindu American organizations in the US, which are tied to those in India, have produced a virulently anti-Muslim rhetoric and hysterical generalizations about 'Islamic terrorism' and Pakistani militants that have overlapped, often intentionally, with the Bush regime's rhetoric in the War on Terror (Kurien 261–288; Menon 55–79). This is, of course, only too apparent in the wake of the attacks in Mumbai, India in November 2008. Communal or religious, as well as national, tensions were apparent in South Asian communities long before they were exacerbated by the events of 9/11 and the War on Terror; religious cleavages, as well as political fissures between Indians, Pakistanis, and

Bangladeshis, were in many cases deepened after 2001. Among the South Asian immigrant youth in the study, however, a pan-Islamic if not also pan-South Asian identification seemed to supersede these differences among Muslim youth from India, Pakistan, and Bangladesh as they formed friendships with other South Asian students and Muslim youth from Morocco or Somalia.

Dissenting feelings

For youth in general, notions of dissent necessarily take forms that may be different from those expressed by adults, for their notions of the state, resistance, or politics are embedded in different developmental and social contexts. Youth are also generally more vulnerable to the state's disciplining power, and do not have all the legal rights of adult citizens. A conversation with a Pakistani immigrant student, Samir, helped me think about the ambiguity of modes of political dissent expressed by South Asian Muslim youth. The incident took place in the International Student Center, a room where immigrant students in the high school bilingual program often hung out between classes and used the computer terminals, since most did not have computers at home. This is an excerpt from my field notes in September 2002:

> I'm in the International Center one morning when Samir comes in and sits down at one of the computer terminals. I ask him if he has a webpage and though Samir is generally a bit quiet, he calls me over excitedly and pulls it up. It has links to 'Lollywood' [Pakistani] films, Bollywood film music, and also to 'funny pictures.' I ask him if I can see these pictures, and when he clicks on the link, pages and pages of pictures of [George] W. [Bush] appear, a row of him wiggling his hips, a row of him looking like a chimpanzee, a row looking like Superman.
>
> 'This is great,' I say, laughing, 'So you think the same thing about Dubya?'
>
> Samir doesn't seem to understand the reference, and he also doesn't respond.
>
> 'So you don't like George Bush?'
>
> 'No,' he says, 'I just saw these and I thought they were funny.'

Then he scrolls down and there is a digitally produced photograph of a bearded Bush looking like Osama [bin Laden] with a white turban coiled around his head, and a picture of the Statue of Liberty draped in a hijab. I ask Samir what he thinks of them and why he chose to put them up, and he simply replies that someone sent them to him. Yet these are the only 'funny' images he has up, and also the only images related to America or to politics. They are clearly, grotesquely, about 9/11 and about George W. Bush.

I spent a long time wondering about Samir's funny pictures, his responses to me, and the political thinking it could imply: was this a vernacular mode of dissenting citizenship? Despite his verbal denial, was Samir placing these images on his website as a way of expressing a coded critique of Bush? The images, obviously, did not collectively produce a consistent critique. The veiled Statue of Liberty reified notions of gender and Islam and evoked anxieties about the transformation of cherished symbols of 'American freedom' by Islam or Muslim fundamentalism, suggesting that what Muslim terrorists or Al Qaeda wanted was to attack the American 'way of life.' In contrast, the image of George W. Bush grinning in a bin-Ladenesque turban played visually with the question of who the 'real' terrorist might be. This image, which digitally 'mashes' together signifiers of the President and 'the terrorist,' implicitly questions Bush's own civilizational discourse of a clash between 'Western' modernity and democracy and Islamic fundamentalism and anti-modernity, suggesting the two are not as sharply dichotomous as this discourse suggests. On a deeper level, the image could also challenge the presumed binary between the rational violence and 'just wars' waged by the US and the irrational violence and militant fanaticism associated with the 9/11 attacks by fusing the two symbols of this clash between 'good' and 'evil.' The caricatures of Bush as chimp or Superman certainly mocked the President's zealous crusade against 'evil.'

Was the website Samir's way of grappling with the anti-Islamic caricatures pervading American popular culture by responding with caricatures of his own choice, resituated on a webpage that was swathed in green and decorated with the Pakistani flag? Or was it simply that Samir thought these images were amusing? Either way, the choice of these pictures did not seem totally accidental but suggestive of an attempt to play with the images of Islam, terrorism, and US power circulating in public and popular culture. 'The political' seeped into his translation of these images via cyberculture, wrapped in his national pride, his Muslim identity, and possibly his own unvocalized feelings about Bush and the War on Terror. The seemingly contradictory juxtaposition of Samir's Pakistani pride and the images of bin Laden and the hijab may not express an explicit or consistent political critique, but they hint at some unease with the dominant discourse about Islam and 'terrorism' and, clearly, a dissenting humor.

This incident was one of the moments involving youth in the study that gave me the most pause, for it made me think about the ways in which young people engage with the political, and the often subtle ways in which they may express a range of responses to questions of power, the state, and resistance. Yet, it is these kinds of moments of ambiguous dissent, potentially expressed from multiple locations and against various forces that are important to consider when thinking about the political subjectivity of youth, especially from groups targeted for political speech. This illustrates what James Scott (137, 152) has described as techniques of resistance of subordinate or repressed groups that infiltrate the 'public transcript' of political discourse in ways that are 'intended to be cryptic and opaque' to escape retaliation by the powerful. Samir's images are perhaps a form of 'hinted blasphemy' that test the limits of what is permissible by a subtle manipulation of political meaning that exists on a continuum of challenges to dominant interpretations of 'terrorism' or 'fundamentalism' by targeted or dissenting groups. The refusal to verbalize political critique is important to note for it shows the many ways this silence is layered with the quiet but charged nuances of 'dissent' and 'complicity.'

If the imperial is a feeling, it is also worthwhile to consider dissent as a 'feeling,' as something that is not simply caught in the binary of resistance and complicity but that is expressed in ambiguous and hard to identify ways, such as Samir's funny pictures. This does not mean giving up on the tangibility of dissent, and the ever pressing need for resistance in the face of state-sponsored violence, or on the difficult and ever lurking danger of complicity. On the contrary, thinking of dissenting feelings allows us to acknowledge the continuum of responses of resistance, especially among those who are coerced into silence by repressive state measures or who are outside of traditional organized movements, while not falling prey to a romanticization of heroic protest or passive victimhood based on familiar tropes. Furthermore, the Internet is not necessarily a space that automatically allows for the expression of dissent or subtle critique, and surveillance of cyberspace after 9/11 has led to cases where the FBI has targeted Muslim youth, such as the astounding case of a Bangladeshi American girl who was deported after participating in Islamic online groups.

Neoliberal citizenship and consumption

It is important not to idealize the possibilities for political expression available to youth through the consumption of media, while exploring how popular culture offers 'symbolic resources' to young people to engage with questions of politics outside of official institutions and political parties and to produce their own understandings of cultural citizenship or dissenting citizenship (Willis 131, 149). The consumption of global media for the youth in this study was restricted by their role as part-time workers in the service economy of the city. Work affected young immigrants' sociality and access to popular culture but they also forged relationships and understood cultural citizenship through work. For example, Walid, who worked in the evenings as a security guard, said:

> When I was in Pakistan, I was thinking of being a cricket player, because I love cricket! I was in a cricket club in Lahore, but now, there's no time to play. You gotta have to work here, we don't have no place to go besides movies and malls. I started going to the YMCA to work out; I'd like to go every day but I don't always have time. And the other thing is, if you want to go meet someone, like your friend, you have a job and he has a different day off. Sometimes on Eid, we get together and we go and chill out. But back home, in Pakistan, you don't have to work and stuff. I work as security in a warehouse near the mall, I go there at nights every weekend.... It's easy, but it's boring.

Walid's reflections on his life in Wellford underscored that work made it very difficult for these immigrant youth to socialize with one another, to hang out in the city, and consume popular culture in public spaces, but this does not imply a neat dichotomy between labor and youth culture. The participation of these young immigrants in US public culture, in fact, was largely mediated by labor and their social relations outside the school and community were primarily with other immigrant or young workers and with employers, often of diverse ethnic and national backgrounds, in the service sector.

Popular culture is an arena in which individual consumer-citizen identities are constructed, a process that shapes how youth grapple with the meanings of citizenship and dissent in their everyday lives. As Nestor García Canclini observes, youth increasingly access notions of the citizen through the form of popular culture, rather than through more traditional avenues based on formal institutions of citizenship or political organizations. If youth are supposedly alienated from traditional, public forms of political participation, so is the vast majority of the populace in a country such as the United States. However, it is important to note that the production of cultural citizenship through the use of cultural commodities is still embedded in relationships with the state and market, both of which are heavily invested in the meanings attached to citizenship by the younger generation. Dissenting citizenship, too, can be commodified and consumed, as in the case of progressive hip hop or anti-war music, not to mention commodities such as T-shirts and buttons.

Cultural consumption is linked to neo-liberal citizenship and for young people, like adults, American neoliberal nationalism is closely tied to a culture of consumption, on many levels. On one level, consumption practices are central to defining one's identity in relation to a collective identity, as well as national culture, and class, racial, and ethnic hierarchies (Maira 134–160; Park). On a broader level, theorists of citizenship point to the emergence of the model of the citizen as consumer with the increasing privatization of services previously offered by the welfare state. Liberal conceptions of individualized citizenship mesh well with the notion of individualized consumption in capitalist democracies, where citizen rights are a form of possessive property (Holston and Appadurai 11; Miller 129–130). Citizenship in the neo-liberal capitalist state means being a productive worker who is not automatically entitled to social services as a citizen but must try to gain access to them as an individual consumer.

Compared to more affluent or highly credentialed South Asian immigrants, these working-class youth are more ambiguously positioned in relation to the US neoliberal ideology of productivity and consumption (Ong 739). These young immigrants and their families came to the US, in a sense, to consume the mythologized promise of the American Dream, but it was often shattered soon after their arrival. In addition to part-time jobs in the service sector, South Asian immigrant youth also worked in their homes – doing childcare or family chores – and for family businesses, work which sometimes fell into the category of unpaid labor and that is not uncommon for youth in general, particularly the children of immigrant entrepreneurs. Soman, an Indian immigrant student, worked in his family's Bengali restaurant in Prospect Square after school and often waited on more affluent South Asian immigrant students from the prestigious university down the street. He said, 'Here, you live in a golden cage, but it's still a cage... my life is so limited. I go to school, come to work, study, go to sleep.' Soman's comment about being imprisoned by the 'golden cage' of the American Dream is profound because in a single image it invokes the glittering appeal of American capitalism and the confining imprisonment not just of the lifestyle it engenders but also of the belief in this illusion.

The US, as well as other states that are 'consumerized republics,' place mass consumption at the center of nation-building (Cohen 9). 'Consumer nationalism,' according to Inderpal Grewal (197, 219–220), collapses classical liberal distinctions between civil society and the market, 'promoting endlessly the idea of choice as central to a liberated subject.' Grewal (206) observes that the notion of 'freedom,' key to Bush's global War on Terror to defend the American 'way of life,' is marketed through American popular culture that circulates globally; '"freedom" as a specific kind of "choice" was created as a symbol of [American] nationalism' through the spread of American consumer culture. The immigrant youth in this study understand themselves as consumers of not just commodities or media but also educational opportunities or the promise of a 'way of life' that compelled their parents to migrate from South Asia. South Asian immigrant youth have limited resources to purchase commodities, but they also engage in the ideological consumption of notions of democracy, representation, or belonging. Many of these immigrant youth had encountered the United States first through Hollywood films; for example, Shireen and another Indian Gujarati girl, Samira, remembered seeing the blockbuster movie, *Titanic*, in their villages and towns in South Asia before they embarked on their own journey to the US. This film, imagining America as the destination of immigrants' dreams and the desires of the young protagonists, in particular, is an example of how the ideology of the American Dream is consumed by young people around the world. The notion of 'choosing' freedom and democracy, presumably over other ways of life and in opposition to those who 'hate' America, is a central tenet of imperial culture and cultures of neoliberalism, shaping as well as constraining possibilities of dissenting citizenship.

Immigrant students were drawn to US popular culture, often before they had set foot in the US, not just due to transnational media but also because of transnational ties that introduced them to new cultural forms or subcultural styles while living in South Asia. For example, Faisal learned basketball while growing up in Pakistan, a country where cricket is by far a more popular national sport, because his father was living in the US for 15 years and introduced him to basketball on his visits home. Some of these immigrant youths had grown up with one foot tenuously planted in subcultures from another part of the world, as a result of the globalization of popular culture and its intersections with the South Asian Diaspora. These immigrant youths understood US cultural citizenship through their consumption of an array of cultural forms, including elements of local or urban US youth subcultures, that are linked to larger imaginings of national belonging. Subcultures can also promote the notion of individual freedom to 'choose' an identity based on style, through purchasing certain kinds of fashion, music, or other commodities, and learning codes of subcultural belonging, thus performing various kinds of consumer citizenship within the landscape of neoliberal capitalism. Immigrant youth in this study formed a subcultural connection with one another based on their shared identification as immigrant, South Asian, and Muslim; they hung out together inside and outside school and shared similar cultural interests in South Asian films and music.

However, there is a perception, in mainstream media, public discourse, and even implicitly, in some academic research that what binds immigrant youth together is the presumed 'culture clash' between 'traditional' family values and 'American' public culture, suggesting that inter-generational conflict is a key element of immigrant youth subcultures. Much has already been written about Muslim immigrant youth straddling 'two worlds,' a trope which frames 'Muslim' and 'American' identities in binary opposition and suggests that this 'culture clash' potentially leads to an 'anti-American' youth culture. Political and cultural tensions about national belonging in the US certainly exist for South Asian Muslim immigrant youth, especially in the post-9/11 moment. Yet the immigrant youth in this study responded to questions of cultural transition in ways that were far more complex, even fluid, than acknowledged in mainstream discourse, especially in discussions of Muslim American youth that are generally tinged to varying degrees with Orientalist notions of binding 'traditions.' The students I spoke to were critical of US foreign policies and of domestic profiling and surveillance of their communities, but this critique of the state co-existed with their desires for cultural citizenship and negotiations with American popular culture in daily life. Discussions of subcultural citizenship for Muslim immigrant youth also need to be situated in relation to ideologies of national belonging that construct any incipient Muslim American youth culture as potentially opposed to Western modernity and questioning of the 'American way of life,' or at least, vulnerable to dissenting political movements that are viewed as a threat to US interests.

Gendering dissent: Good, moderate, and bad Muslims

The fashioning of Muslim American youth subcultures also has a gendered meaning, but one that is often distorted in the public imagination; there is a reified construction of Muslim-ness in relation to youth that divorces Muslim youth from the complexity of the range of youth cultures and political issues with which they are engaged. Much of the discourse in the mainstream media about Muslim youth in the US, after 9/11 but also well before, has tended to dwell on the image of fanatical boys and girls wearing hijab, generally producing an Orientalist notion of Muslim youth bound by an unchanging religion and completely outside of modern (i.e. 'Western' or American) youth culture.

Performances of cultural citizenship by Muslim American youth are shaped by religion, class, nationalism, and also gender, through an uneasy conjoining of liberalism, feminism, and Orientalism. A particular space has been constructed for Muslim and Arab women in the post-9/11 debate about the War on Terror that is very revealing of the ways in which Muslim-ness, and also Arab-ness, is gendered in the public sphere. In the high school, for example, more South Asian Muslim girls than boys spoke at public events in the aftermath of 9/11, even though the boys were the most visible targets of profiling (most Muslim girls in the school did not wear hijab). The issue of visibility or hyper-visibility of Muslim girls and women is evident in the need for, and production of, spokespersons for Islam who increasingly circulate in the US media, generally speaking about the issue of women's rights in Islam and in Arab or South Asian societies. This raises questions about the gendering of cultural citizenship, for US imperial interventions are legitimized through a discourse of liberating Muslim women and US liberal feminism is preoccupied with rescuing women in hijab or presumably 'oppressed' Muslim women in order to bring them into the fold of the nation. At the same time, there is a deep anxiety about Muslim men, especially young males, as potential terrorists and religious fanatics who are, unlike women perhaps, ultimately inassimilable. As Miriam Cooke (9) observes, 'Imperial logic genders and separates subject peoples so that the men are the Other and the women are civilizable.'

Gendered performances of dissenting citizenship are embedded in distinctions between 'good' and 'bad' Muslims that are defined according to the state's interests in regulating Muslim subjects that support or oppose its policies, as suggested by Mahmood Mamdani (15). 'Good citizenship' or 'moderate' Muslim politics was performed by Muslim Americans after 9/11 in a variety of ways, testifying loyalty to the nation and asserting belief in its democratic ideals, as evident in the performances of some female spokespersons and other so-called moderate Muslim commentators, such as Asra Nomani and Fareed Zakaria (Maira '"Good" and "Bad" Muslim Citizens'; see Dabashi 'Native Informers'). Young Muslim immigrants, too, quickly become attuned to the registers in which political dissent is expressed in a repressive political climate, which for 'moderate' Muslims rests on affirming Islam as a religion of peace and disavowing terrorism; Steven Salaita (50–51) describes this mandatory disclaimer the 'prerequisite to speaking' for Muslims in the public sphere. The desire to perform 'good' Muslim citizenship has altered the identities and social relations within Muslim American communities after 9/11, and created divisiveness, mistrust, and suspicion related to questions of dissent and complicity.

The notion of good Muslim citizenship also dovetails with a rhetoric of multicultural inclusion that emphasizes liberal 'tolerance' of religious difference, via a form of religious multiculturalism. Orientalist constructions of 'the Muslim world' reinscribe the multiculturalist presumption that political injustice can be resolved simply by awareness of religious or cultural 'diversity,' ignoring the larger geo-political and imperial frames of the War on Terror. Muslim American youth are often forced to become token representatives of Islam for the American public, giving speeches at their schools and in community forums about Islam or participating in interfaith dialogues, but without always being able to raise their concerns about wars or occupations that impact their communities and countries of origin. Furthermore, focusing on 'Muslim' as just another cultural (or ambiguously racial) marker has, in some cases, absorbed Arab/South Asian/Muslim Americans into a multicultural discourse of difference and belonging and subsumed the category 'Muslim' into an ethnicized US identity politics. 'Muslim Americans,' or the trio of 'Arab, Muslim, and South Asian Americans' (AMSA is the label used by some community activists after 9/11), are constructed as belonging to just another, culturally distinct ethnic category whose problems can be contained within a discourse of domestic racism and addressed by inclusion within the multicultural nation (see Alsultany 593–622).

While it is evident that the disciplining or exclusion of Muslim Americans rests on a form of racial thinking that legitimizes their eviction from political community, as argued by Sherene Razack, it is also apparent that the assault on civil liberties after 9/11 needs to be linked to US strategic interests and overseas interventions in the Middle East and South Asia and also to a longer history of anti-Arab racism in the US, which is related to US support for Israel and desire for hegemony in the Middle East. The War on Terror has highlighted the limitations of liberal multiculturalism as a response to state policies targeting Muslim and Arab Americans after 9/11, as it evades the larger political context and deeper structural racism undergirding Islamophobia as well as anti-Arab racism. Some Muslim Americans, as I found in my research on immigrant youth, absorbed the liberal discourse of multiculturalism pervasive in the high school but simultaneously understood the anti-Muslim backlash in relation to other forms of subjugation, racialization, and repression in the US and also globally, including anti-Muslim violence in South Asia, and began forging cross-ethnic or inter-racial affiliations and alliances based on a deeper critique of oppression and marginality (Maira *Missing*).

Conclusion

This essay touches on some ways in which issues of dissent and citizenship for South Asian Muslim immigrant youth after 9/11 intersect with questions of youth culture and cultural consumption and are inflected by issues of class and gender. Questions of national belonging or cultural citizenship for these youth are deeply shaped by the political forces of a particular global project, that of US imperial power, and by the biopolitics of neoliberal capitalism. These issues are often missing in work on Muslim American youth in the US, which has tended to focus rather narrowly on questions of culture, religion, and gender, without sufficiently taking into account issues of labor, popular culture, or political dissent. At the same time, the it is important to keep in mind the limitations and contradictions of dissenting citizenship, as a mode of critique that is still harnessed to the state, and the problems of a religious multiculturalism that stresses liberal tolerance while evading imperial policies. The dissent of groups that are targeted by the state has to be understood in the larger context of what political resistance might look like in a climate of repression, and what this might mean for South Asian communities in the US as they various resist, ignore, or conform to the disciplining power of the imperial state.

Notes

1. The 2000 Census reported 2720 Indian immigrants (2.7% of the population), 125 Pakistanis, and 120 Bangladeshis in Wellford, a city that is 68.1% White American, 11.9% African American, 11.9% Asian American, and 7.4% Latino (US Census Bureau). This, of course, does not include undocumented immigrants. The 'native' population is 74.1% and foreign-born is 25.9%; 17.7% are not citizens and 31.2% speak a language other than English. Wellford is of course skewed by the presence of the academic community; while 8.2% (3108) of those enrolled in schools are in high school, fully 70.5% are in college or graduate school, and 38.5% of the population over 25 years has a graduate or professional degree.
2. The high school had approximately 2000 students, of which about 40% were white and the remaining 60% were students of color. African Americans were the largest group of students of color (about 25%), followed by Latinos (15%), and Asian Americans (about 7%). In the year I was doing my field work, there were about 60 students of South Asian origin in the high school, evenly split between immigrant students and second-generation youth.
3. This study is based on interviews with South Asian Muslim immigrant students, as well as with second-generation South Asian youth and other Muslim immigrant students, parents of immigrant and non-immigrant students, teachers, staff, youth program organizers, community and religious leaders, and immigrant and civil rights activists. I also did field work in a range of sites in Wellford and in the area, in addition to the school, such as homes, workplaces, social gatherings, and cultural and political events.

References

Agamben, Giorgio. *State of Exception*. Trans. Kevin Attell. Chicago and London: U of Chicago P, 2005. Print.

Alsultany, Evelyn. "Selling American Diversity and Muslim American Identity through Nonprofit Advertising Post-9/11." *American Quarterly* 59.3 (2007): 593–622. Print.

Appadurai, Arjun. *Modernity at Large: Cultural Dimensions of Globalization*. Minneapolis: U of Minnesota P, 1996. Print.

Basch, Linda, Nina Glick Schiller, and Cristina Szanton Blanc, eds. *Nations Unbound: Transnational Projects, Postcolonial Predicaments, and Deterritorialized Nation-States*. Amsterdam: Gordon and Breach, 1994. Print.

Canclini, Nestór García. *Consumers and Citizens: Globalization and Multicultural Conflicts*. Minneapolis: U of Minnesota P, 2001. Print.

Cohen, Lizabeth. *A Consumer's Republic: The Politics of Mass Consumption in Postwar America*. New York: Knopf, 2003. Print.

Cooke, Miriam. "Islamic Feminism Before and After September 11." *Duke Journal of Gender Law and Policy* 227.9 (2002). Web. 11 Mar. 2008. <http://find.galegroup.com/itx/infomark.do?&contentSet=3DIAC-Documents&type=3Dretrieve&tabID=3DT002&prodId=3DEAIM&docId=3DA90988303&source=3Dgale&user=GroupName=3Ducdavis&version=3D1.0>.

Dabashi, Hamid. "Native Informers and the Making of the American Empire." *Al-Ahram Weekly* 2006. Web. 16 Nov. 2006. <http://weekly.ahram.org.eg/print/2006/797/special.htm>.

France, Alan. "'Why Should We Care?': Young People, Citizenship and Questions of Social Responsibility." *Journal of Youth Studies* 1.1 (1998): 97–111. Print.

Ganguly, Keya. *States of Exception: Everyday Life and Postcolonial Identity*. Minneapolis: U of Minnesota P, 2001.

Grewal, Inderpal. *Transnational America: Feminisms, Diasporas, Neoliberalisms*. Durham, NC: Duke UP, 2005. Print.

Hansen, Thomas B., and Finn Steputat. "Introduction." *Sovereign Bodies: Citizens, Migrants, and States in the Postcolonial World*. Ed. Thomas B. Hansen and Finn Steputat. Princeton: Princeton UP, 2005. 1–36. Print.

Hardt, Michael, and Antonio Negri. *Empire*. Cambridge, MA: Harvard UP, 2000. Print.

Hindess, Barry. "Citizenship and Empire." *Sovereign Bodies: Citizens, Migrants, and States in the Postcolonial World*. Ed. Thomas B. Hansen and Finn Steputat. Princeton: Princeton UP, 2005. 241–56. Print.

Holston, James, and Arjun Appadurai. "Introduction: Cities and Citizenship." *Cities and Citizenship*. Ed. James Holston. Durham: Duke UP, 1999. 1–18. Print.

Kaplan, Amy, and Donald Pease, eds. *Cultures of United States Imperialism*. Durham: Duke UP, 1993. Print.

Kurien, Prema. "To Be or Not to Be South Asian: Contemporary Indian American Politics." *Journal of Asian American Studies* 6.3 (2003): 261–88. Print.

Maira, Sunaina. "Temporary Tattoos: Indo-Chic Fantasies and Late Capitalist Orientalism." *Meridians: Feminism, Race, Transnationalism* 3.1 (2000): 134–60. Print.

Maira, Sunaina. *Missing: Youth, Citizenship, and Empire After 9/11*. Durham, NC: Duke UP, 2009. Print.

Maira, Sunaina. "'Good' and 'Bad' Muslim Citizens: Feminists, Terrorists and US Orientalisms." *Feminist Studies* 35.3 (2009): 631–56. Print.

Maira, Sunaina, and Elisabeth Soep, eds. "Introduction." *Youthscapes: The Popular, the National, the Global*. Philadelphia: Temple UP, 2005. 15–35. Print.

Mamdani, Mahmood. *Good Muslim, Bad Muslim: America, the Cold War, and the Roots of Terror*. New York: Pantheon, 2004. Print.

Menon, Sridevi. "Where is West Asia in Asian America? 'Asia' and the Politics of Space in Asian America." *Social Text* 24.1 (2006): 55–79. Print.

Miller, Toby. *The Well-Tempered Subject: Citizenship, Culture, and the Postmodern Subject*. Baltimore: The Johns Hopkins UP, 1993.

Ong, Aihwa. "Cultural Citizenship as Subject-Making: Immigrants Negotiate Racial and Cultural Boundaries in the United States." *Current Anthropology* 37.5 (1996): 737–62. Print.

Park, Lisa S. *Consuming Citizenship: Children of Asian Immigrant Entrepreneurs*. Stanford, CA: Stanford UP, 2005. Print.

Pease, Donald. "New Perspectives on U.S. Culture and Imperialism." *Cultures of United States Imperialism*. Ed. Amy Kaplan and Donald Pease. Durham: Duke UP, 1993. 22–37. Print.

Razack, Sherene H. *Casting Out: The Eviction of Muslims from Western Law and Politics*. Toronto: U of Toronto P, 2008. Print.

Román, Ediberto. "Membership Denied: An Outsider's Story of Subordination and Subjugation Under U.S. Colonialism." *Moral Imperialism: A Critical Anthology*. Ed. Berta E. Hernández-Truyol. New York: New York UP, 2002. 269–84. Print.

Robin, Corey. *Fear: The History of a Political Idea*. New York: Oxford UP, 2004. Print.

Rothschild, Matthew. *You Have No Rights; Stories of America in an Age of Repression*. New York: New Press, 2007. Print.

Salaita, Steven. *Anti-Arab Racism in the USA*. London: Pluto Press, 2006.

Scott, James C. *Domination and the Arts of Resistance: Hidden Transcripts*. New Haven: Yale UP, 1990. Print.

Stoler, Ann L. "Intimidations of Empire: Predicaments of the Tactile and Unseen." *Haunted by Empire: Geographies of Intimacy in North American History*. Ed. Ann L. Stoler. Durham, NC: Duke UP, 2006. 1–22. Print.

US Census Bureau. *United States Census 2000*. n.d. Web. <http://www.census.gov/main/www/cen2000.html>.

Williams, William A. *Empire as a Way of Life: An Essay on the Causes and Character of America's Present Predicament*. New York: Oxford UP, 1980. Print.

Willis, Paul. *Common Culture: Symbolic Work at Play in the Everyday Cultures of the Young*. Milton Keynes, UK: Open UP, 1990. Print.

Global nationalisms, pastoral identities: Association for India's Development (AID) negotiates transnational activism

Kumarini Silva

Department of Communication Studies, Northeastern University, Boston, MA 02115, USA

Acknowledging that AID's work is influential – and that it has a large following within the diasporic and expatriate community in the United States and India – this essay shows how the language and practice of 'giving back' under a rubric of liberal multiculturalism and humanism is still deeply steeped in neoliberal discourses and practices that make assumptions about power, individual agency, and privacy. Classified as a country with 'soft currency,' India is dependent on the very economic exchanges – such as free market trading and the outsourcing of labor to the West – against which the organization structures its philosophy. Such contradictions exist side by side, and the identities that emerge from these contradictions are what this research defines as global nationalism and pastoral identities.

Introduction

'We must be doing *something* if you want to do your research on us,' Sami[1] tells me as we walk over to sit at a table. I tell him that dissertations, once complete, spend their lives in relative obscurity so he should not put much stock in my request. The humor is lost on Sami as he shakes his head 'no' and reiterates that academic work on AID must mean that it is 'on the map.' Our conversation was taking place in the early part of 2002 at one of the annual general meetings of the Association for India's Development (AID) in San Francisco, California. Sami is a typical AID activist: he is originally from India, has a master's degree in electrical engineering, and works for a large technology company in the bay area. Our conversation is peppered with language that I will hear over and over again throughout the following days. Words like 'development from below,' 'under globalization,' and 'give back.' Indeed, giving back to India is the mantra for the movement. AID started out, in 1991, as a small group of Indian students – attending university in the US – who wanted to 'give back' to India through social activism. The organization grew to include a diverse population that included the aforementioned students as well as a large diasporic community, and was incorporated in 2003. Now, with 36 chapters in the United States, and over 1000 members, AID has carried out hundreds of projects in various states in India.[2]

Straddling both the United States – where the bulk of the fundraising occurs – and India – where all the projects are implemented, AID retains an international flair in its fundraising and members, while espousing a commitment to an indigenous model of development that attempts to transcend the economic, political, and socio-cultural challenges of India. Acknowledging that AID's work is influential – and that it has a large following within the diasporic and expatriate community in the United States and India – this essay shows how the language and practice of 'giving back' under a rubric of liberal multiculturalism and humanism is still deeply steeped in neoliberal discourses and practices that make assumptions about power, individual agency, and privacy. It is a neoliberal discourse that neither challenges systemic relations of power, class and caste, nor offers a critique of liberal secularism from a dominant Hindu perspective.

This neoliberal approach to activism allows the organization to construct their diasporic and expatriate selves as a monolith and India as homogenous nation. Within this simplistic binary, where heterogeneity within both community and country are obfuscated, the activist relationship is constructed through an affective relationship between US-based economic success, *vis-à-vis* the non-resident-Indian (NRI), and diasporic nostalgia and longing for a 'homeland.' Classified as a country with 'soft currency,' India is dependent on the very economic exchanges – such as free market trading and the outsourcing of labor to the West – against which the organization structures its philosophy. Such contradictions exist side by side, and the identities that emerge from these contradictions are what this research defines as *global nationalism* and *pastoral identities*. The contradictions serve a useful purpose because they allow the organization to partake in a globalized world, while still claiming a specific socio-cultural and geo-political space in which to mobilize. In this context, a global nationalism manifests through the diasporic imaginings of people working on behalf of a secular homeland – a nationalistic ethos that defies the realities of divided communities and ethnic violence that is the legacy of colonialism. As part of this, pastoral identities – constructing the country and people through pastoralized depictions of community and community building, discussed at length below – become the narrative for this cohesive identity.

Imagining India through the Diaspora

As a transnational movement that straddles both the United States and India, AID articulates both lived realities on local levels, and constructed and mythologized identities of nation that circulate on the global level. These realities are sutured together, creating complex and contested identities. Such contestations are not unusual to the Diaspora, where longing (for the pastoral home), belonging (within the 'new' space), and memory (the imagining of home, both past and present) are deeply interwoven (see Hua 191–208; Agnew 23–47; Chakrabarty; Morse 63–74). In addition to these affective relationships, US identifications such as 'resident alien,' 'F-1 student,' 'J-1 Tourist,' all contribute to how India is evoked as a place of belonging – as home – among the non-resident Indians. Many of them are first and second generation Americans of Indian heritage that have never been to India.[3] Nevertheless, they are committed to and continue to work for an India that is – as a cultural, social, and geo-political space – conceived of as 'home' – whether it is theirs or their parents'. For many, the conditions of living in a country where they are not recognized as part of the majority results in a connection to a 'motherland,' whether it be real, mythic or constructed. For some, it is the possibility of 'going back' – returning to a space that is their own where they imagine they will not function as second class citizens – that motivates their activism (for a more lengthy discussion of this, see Silva 693–706). While this alienation from US society is not openly discussed, and few may recognize it, conversations with activists,[4] both Indians and Indian Americans in the US, reveal it. This feeling of simultaneous alienation and marginal acceptance has a profound effect on how India is constructed as a nation, the vision *for* this constructed India, and the role envisioned by the organization for its activists.

These various issues are revealed through interviews carried out with activists in the US and in the responses to presentations at the AID conference held in San Francisco in 2002. During many of the presentations at the conference, transnational corporations were critiqued for exploiting India, and this critique met with resounding support from the audience. Following this, during personal interviews with members of that audience, it was revealed that many worked for transnational corporations similar to those that were criticized. When questioned about this contradiction, the response was that their time in the US was intended to earn money and to benefit from a globalized economy so that they could move back to India and work *for* India, thus separating 'western' economic success from the bucolic imaginings of 'home,' even though, in practice, they are deeply intertwined and inseparable. It is at this intersection that the rhetoric of neoliberalism most powerfully emerges. As one activist[5] noted:

> We are all educated, and we believe that by educating others we can bring them to our levels, prosperity, whatever you want to call it ... organizations like AID tell you, you can channel your energies to do something for India ... we all come here [to the US] and we are doing reasonably well, right? And we all want to help ... there is a geographical distance and we can see the problems within it ... so these organizations [like AID] provide infrastructure to do something constructive ... I may not agree with all their ideologies but if it gives me an opportunity to do something that brings me satisfaction.

The desire of 'we' who are educated and doing reasonably well to bring 'them to our levels' articulates a naturalized relationship between development, human rights, welfare state biopolitics, and economics (Cooper 9). Moreover, within this structure, the activism and participation in AID becomes a form of self-satisfaction or 'self care' (Brown 42): to fulfill one's own desires and patriotic energies – to give back what has been given – from a distance. This desire to connect to India from afar, and the ethical and moral responsibility of this connection, is echoed by one of AID's founding members. When asked about his reasons for co-founding AID, he responds:

> Life is compartmentalized, right? ... like family ... I'm studying and I'm going to be working and this is what I'm doing for my family and so on. But I kind of thought that no matter what, we all should do everything ... as Indians we all talk a lot about, you know, the problems and challenges in India. And we are concerned also.... In India we are absolutely speaking of a very small part of the cities we know... even while we are here, and no matter which stage we are in life, whether we are a student or working, whether it be here or back in India – we should be able to connect with the villages.[6]

Here again, the pastoralized vision of a 'village' is evoked as the locus of India – the real India. Furthermore, evoking 'Indians' as a homogenous community rather than a heterogeneous multiplicity made up of different religions, ethnic and linguistic identities, and classes and castes, erases culturally-based structural inequalities from the societies that exist in the actual geo-political space that is India. It allows the community living *outside* this space to come together – also as a homogenous group – for its greater good as an example for the possibilities of India. On another level, the ethnic, religious and caste differences are articulated within a rural/urban dichotomy that is more acceptable as a trope of uneven development. This discursive connection to the pastoral village, the rural poor, remains central to AID's identity and ideology. The poor are seen as backbone of the nation – the proletariat. The rural poor of India are evoked as a *condition*, rather than a community. The *community* itself is *all* Indians – living in India, in the United States, and other non-resident Indians – while the *conditions* of poverty are experienced by some. So in order to remedy the condition, the hope is to form alliances between those who have, and those who do not. Thus, the village remains central to this neoliberal imagining of nation as a nexus for making connections and solidifying belonging – by connecting with the village, you can connect with the 'true' nation – a dated nationalist trope that evokes *swadeshi*.[7]

Indeed, the tropes of nationalism evoked by the US-based activists, as well as the activism in the United States, speak to a pastoralized mono-ethnic identity that is evoked – whether one has a tangible connection *vis-à-vis* an immediate family in India or is a second generation American with Indian parents – as patriotic belonging. By using Indian cultural events and constructing India as a mother and lover rhetorically, AID connects its members *and* its donors to a united India that belongs to them all. The *cultural* connection is constantly evoked as a common history, because the actual canonical history of India remains a contested and uncomfortable space. This cultural construction of territorial identities is not unusual. As Negus and Roman-Velazquez note, identities built on cultural forms and social practices are 'profoundly territorial: we locate ourselves with reference to a nation, region, city, neighborhood; we use concepts of class, race or ethnicity that imply certain correspondence between members of groups and localities and points of origin' (331).

In interviews carried out with AID members in the United States, this correspondence to 'points of origin' was clearly visible. In one conversation, a young activist noted that he got involved with the organization because he felt he had very little understanding of his Indian heritage in any true sense of the word and thought this would be a good opportunity to 'help India' and also get in touch with his roots. He states,

> I have never been there, you know, and I was thinking that maybe by getting involved and doing something with AID I would be able to resolve this conflict. I'm planning to go back [laugh] okay, not 'go back' because I've never been there, but go there next summer and do some work or something.[8]

This desire to 'go back' to a space that has never been visited, but has been evoked via participation and imagery is a constant within this community. India is imagined as a very real and tangible place, constructed outside the West where the activists live – and in many cases, have never left. Moreover, if there are fractures, then it is considered up to the people of the Diaspora to reconnect the various communities together, to bring about change. For example, at the 2002 AID conference in San Francisco, an invited speaker at a presentation[9] stated,

> We think it's very, very important for people outside of India to be engaged in struggles in India.... Most of us are Indians and Indian-Americans. We actually occupy a special space politically speaking and socially speaking ... in this larger scheme of things, and by that what I mean is that we are – most of us here are – classified by the Indian government as the NRI community, the non-resident Indian community.... And the Indian government actually looks to us a lot, and in many times has bent over backwards, gives us a lot of preferences, to get things done in India.... They especially look to this community here in the United States ... they target their outreach especially to get investment from the Indian community ... we need to engage this crowd much more....

This call to come together as a 'special' group that politically and socially carries weight to change the socio-cultural, and economic conditions of an India that is being exploited by the 'West' is echoed through out the organizational rhetoric and ideology. According to the movement, this is an exploitation not only of material resources but also an exploitation and importation of people and manpower from India.[10] Responding to this, not only was a special session titled 'Reversing the Brain Drain' included in the 2001 AID conference, the organization also has a *Jeevan Saathi* program – which provides support for US-based volunteers in India – to 'enable and encourage AID volunteers to return to India.'[11]

This 'return' to India is significant, because some returnees, like the American volunteer who inadvertently refers to his first visit as 'going back,' have never been to India. Yet, the desire to move there, to help, to negotiate cultural, social and political spaces that have been outside of their realities, remains strong. These spaces remain outside the realities of these activists not only because they are geographically distant, but also because the communities – mainly rural and low-income areas – that AID works with on a grassroots level are far removed from the realities of its US-based members. Again, AID articulates this disparity as rooted in material resources, rather than cultural or socio-political issues. A lack of access to these resources is, in this discourse, the primary impediment to a self-identified development – or 'globalization from below,' as the activists refer to their grassroots efforts. Even though the majority of the AID volunteers are middle to upper-middle – and even upper-class – Indians living in the United States, India and its poor, as a collective, remain a core narrative. This image of an India that can belong to all if only the urban elite and the rural poor can connect is made most visible through the public rhetoric of the organization. For example, on the front page of a 2001 issue of *Dishaa*, the AID newsletter, emphasized text reads

> When every person of Indian origin in the metros of the US is willing to identify with the simple forest-dwelling Indians, When every Indian software expert is willing to give and take from the India organic farmer, When the children of urban middle classes, the children of the Narmada Valley and the children weaving carpets in Bihar, all wake up in safe and secure homes, then we can say with conviction Mera Bharat Mahaan, That will be the Dawn of a New Era after the long night of freedom.[12]

This vision of a domesticated utopia both rationalizes the group's neoliberal vision of development and preserves existing structural inequalities and differences in ethnicity, religion, language, class and caste. It does so by postulating an underlying, liberal, universal 'Indian' subjectivity that orders and manages these differences as if they were of no consequence to development. 'Safe and secure homes' are the goal of development. Here, India is constructed as a stable but wounded space in need of healing by the diasporic community in the United States. Through the motivations and longings of this community, AID engages in its activism constructing India as one nation far away from a geography that is riddled by separatist politics. The call is *always* to come together as one. Through their campaigns and brochures – such as the end of year fundraiser named 'One for India' where activists are asked to come together as 'one' to raise one dollar a day for India[13] – the organization promotes the idea of a united India, committed to a development that connects the rural to the urban. Since this imagined community is constructed transnationally, rather than locally, it flourishes as a collective 'cause,' and comes out of the desire to negate a history that is antithetical to the indigenous progress that the movement espouses. AID attempts to encourage activism by calling on the collective, pastoralized imagination of the diasporic community. Within this community India becomes a space where ethnicity, religion and caste become immaterial and the 'cause' becomes India-as-a-nation rather than individual politics. In its call to the overseas community, AID states

> Your voice counts... if you can hear the voices of the people – farmers, adivasis, fishworkers, garment workers,... everywhere are struggling for their rights, which are increasingly threatened by a model of development that strengthens the hands of the large, often multinational corporations.... It is assumed that the NRI may be willing to donate money to help alleviate poverty in India but has no quarrel with the overall system nor time to

comment on particular events. At Association for India's Development, we believe in speaking up in favour of sustainable development policy, against exploitation and destruction of livelihoods, to protect human rights and natural resources. Make your voice resonate with the voices of the people.[14]

The rhetoric here constructs the non-resident Indians (NRI) as empowered subjects, who are morally obliged to connect to – and speak for – 'the people' through the discourses of sustainable development, human rights, and management of natural resources. Since the Indian government privileges, according to the organization, the NRI, AID responds by trying to connect the NRI to India through the pathos of nationalism, and civic duty. However, it preserves the 'overall system' that it claims to reject. It simultaneously evokes and deconstructs privilege through nationalistic discourses of belonging. Thus, far from the lived realities of life in India, for the Diaspora, India is constructed as a singular entity. It is the responsibility of *all* Indians – a monolithic amalgam identified only through a constructed nationality rather than citizenship – to work for the greater good of India. However, the reality of India is that it is a space of conflict and contention. As discussed below, the lived experiences of people in India are different from the imaginings of a diaspora.

Imagining India as a geo-political space

In reaction to the rising communal unrest among various religious and ethnic groups in India, many of the AID volunteers wonder how their activism, and AID, can respond to these events. According to grassroots activists, many of the challenges to successful activism are a result of the socio-political climate within the country. As one activist noted,

If you look at communalism [the government] has constructed an alternate history across ... it is a popular alternate history, not an academic one. This alternate history is popular today ... if you talk to a person on the street corner this is the history they will give you. Unless we can reach them at a popular level, that is where we need to start.[15]

Here the state is blamed for constructing and disseminating the flames of communalism through everyday life and culture to an uneducated mass – the person on the street. Therefore, within the actual nation – the geography of India and the lived realties of everyday life – India cannot be constructed as a united, singular socio-cultural space.

In contrast to the diasporic community within AID – where the vernacular language is English, and culture, rather than religion, seems to be the core – grassroots activists are forced to confront the communal conflicts that negate the simple urban elite/rural poor binary. Reflecting this, at the 2002 conference, a much debated and contested discussion on communalism – meaning communal conflict–and its impact on AID took place. US-based activists, simultaneously removed from the actual violence, but ideologically more involved in the realities of 'home,' were concerned about whether AID must and should take a stand against communalism and identify as a secular organization, reflecting the desire for a secular community. A public discussion ensued:

Speaker one:[16] With all the communal violence in Gujarat, it has brought to the forefront the divisiveness of violence. We are having to face it ... while I know that AID is secular, I think it is important for AID to think about projects or encourage seminars on secularism or have interfaith seminars and events. Because if we do not tackle it face on, it is going to determine our agenda ... it is better for us to face it and take it...

For this activist, the reiteration of secularism – as, in this context, an acceptance of all faiths – on the part of AID is crucial as a response to the civil unrest. Her articulations on the need for secularism reiterate this belief in a *homogenous multiculturalism* that is common to AID's activism. She is supported by a second speaker who, unconsciously, evokes colonization as the reason for the current socio-political crisis in India.

> *Speaker two:*[17] Religion is a personal issue ... we grow up with certain values we learn in our families... as you move out you have individual values and community values ... what is happening now is people are forcing their values on others, there are so many missionaries, we can take so many examples ... that is what secularism doesn't propagate ... we should live and let live.

The current civil unrest is seen as 'recent' and 'new' and a condition of the 'missionaries.' Within this ideology the missionaries, rather than local politics and socio-cultural difference, emerges as the 'problem.' As a third speaker directly asks whether they should 'formally adopt a stand on secularism?'[18] a fourth speaker responds to him by reconnecting to the idea of a homogenous multiculturalism and the ideology of 'can't we just get along.'

> *Speaker four:*[19] When we work with organizations and chapters ... we learn as children ... when we deal with an organization we could tell them to teach a special session for communal harmony. Especially telling children that there are good thing in all religions....

By comparing India to a child, taking care of it and raising it to be a caring, compassionate individual becomes the responsibility of AID. In order to fulfill this responsibility, the desire is to always establish a common understanding – the lowest common denominator – of what India is, bringing it back to India as a collective with a rich and vibrant culture, rather than cultures in ethnic and religious conflict. India then is imagined within the framework of an a-historical purity and discourse of childhood, rather than an old history of contention. However, this is not without challenge. In response to speaker four, a fifth speaker states, 'I agree, but we can't eradicate what religion and caste is ... it starts from us ... there is nothing wrong with being a religion ... I appreciate our culture, but I don't think we need to raise religion ... that should be behind closed doors.'[20]

This discourse highlights internal issues of individual and group identity within the organization. While the conversation is about *how* to approach the idea of communalism and secularism and identify in relation to, or in negation of, these terms, the conversation is always foregrounded in terms of what is best for India, rather than for specific communities and individual identities. Speaker five, who states that she 'appreciates the culture,' also stated that this appreciation – which she thought was a sentiment shared by all – should come across through various cultural and social events that highlight *India*, rather than religious values. Her sentiments are not far from how the overall organization does construct India as well as its own identity. While the issue of how one addresses the civil unrest within the country is debated amongst the activists, overall, AID as a collective promotes itself as a movement committed to an India that is united through culture rather than religion.

Conclusion

Rajendra Singh posits that unlike movements of the past, contemporary social movements are heterogeneous, reflecting diverse goals, ideas, views and purposes that speak to changing cultural and social values. According to Singh, in the past society's capacity for reproduction, rejuvenation, and progress was determined by a 'meta-social guarantee of social order, divine rule, natural laws, historical evolution, including the meta-social characteristics of the notion of modernity of the recent past' (102). The deconstruction of such a universal (historical) knowledge in contemporary society has allowed new movements to emerge where 'the forms of social action and movements are plural, following many paths, pursuing different ends and articulating different interests' (Singh 102). This sense of individuality, of determining contextually the solutions to problems that are seen as central to the well-being of civil society, defines new social movements. As such, AID is emblematic of the characteristics that Singh describes. AID is not a static organization and their imaginings of their nation, therefore, are dynamic.

Established under the rubric of Mahatma Gandhi's call for 'Sarvodaya' – which can be loosely translated to 'awakening for all' – AID seeks to empower and develop their country and communities on their own terms. Nevertheless, these categories of country, community and development are terms that have multiple meanings, contexts and functions. The emergence of a movement like AID is an interesting signifier of the processes of negotiating the intersection of history, activism, culture and identity. It speaks to narratives of belonging, dislocation, and relocation created through transnational movements and diasporic longing. As both the organization and the activists negotiate their identities as dynamic processes, influenced by multiple locations and global shifts, they become emblematic of the socio-cultural and political negotiations that influence and give rise to transnational discourses of identity formation.

Notes

1. Names have been changed for privacy.
2. http://www.aidindia.org/hq/chapters/index.htm
3. Based on interviews with various activists at the AID Annual General Meeting held in San Francisco, 25–27 May 2002.
4. Ibid.
5. Interview with US-based male activist on 26 May 2002 at the AID Annual General Meeting in San Francisco.
6. Interview in San Francisco, 26 May 2002.
7. Indigenous or local self-sufficiency.
8. Interview with US-based male activist at the AID Annual General Meeting in San Francisco, 27 May 2002.
9. AID activist who is also part of 'Corpwatch,' an organization that studies the negative impact of corporations across the globe. Presentation given on 27 May 2002 at the AID Annual General Conference in San Francisco.
10. Discussed during various presentations at the 2002 AID conference and also in the decade report published by AID in 2002.
11. AID Decade Report – 1991–2001, p. 8.
12. http://www.aidindia.org/hq/publications/dishaa.htm
13. http://oneforindia.org
14. http://www.aidindia.org/hq/misc/vcounts/voice_counts.html
15. Interview with senior administrator of AID in Chennai, India on 16 December 2002.
16. Female activist based in the United States.
17. Female activist based in the United States.
18. Male activist based in the United States.
19. Female activist based in the United States.
20. Female activist based in the United States.

References

Agnew, Vijay. "Language Matters." *Diaspora, Memory, and Identity: A Search for Home*. Ed. Vijay Agnew. Toronto: U of Toronto P, 2005. 23–47. Print.

Brown, Wendy. *Edge Work: Critical Essays on Knowledge and Politics*. Princeton and Oxford: Princeton UP, 2005. Print.

Chakrabaty, Dipesh. *Habitations of Modernity: Essays in the Wake of Subaltern Studies*. Chicago: U of Chicago P, 2002. Print.

Cooper, Melinda. *Life as Surplus: Biotechnology and Capitalism in the Neoliberal Era*. Seattle and London: U of Washington P, 2008. Print.

Hua, Anh. "Diaspora and Cultural Memory." *Diaspora, Memory, and Identity: A Search for Home*. Ed. Vijay Agnew. Toronto: U of Toronto P, 2005. 191–208. Print.

Morse, Margaret. "Home: Smell, Taste, Posture, Gleam." *Exile, Homeland: Film, Media, and the Politics of Place*. London and New York: Routledge, 1991. 63–74. Print.

Negus, Keith, and Patria Roman-Velazquez, P. "Globalization and Cultural Identities." *Mass Media and Society*. Ed. James Curran and Michael Gurevitch. London: Arnold, 2000. 329–45. Print.

Silva, Kumarini. "Oh, Give Me a Home: Diasporic Longings of Home and Belonging." *Social Identities* 15.5 (2009): 693–706. Print.

Singh, Rajendra. *Social Movements, Old and New*. New Delhi: Sage Publications, 2001. Print.

Impact of tsunami in the East – Muslim women's perspective

Shreen Saroor

Mannar Women Development Federation, Colombo, Sri Lanka

The coastal belt of the east was hit hard by the 2004 Boxing Day tsunami and worst affected were the Muslims who faced marginalization in the post-tsunami reconstruction. The women of this community faced more divergent challenges in the immediate aftermath and in the subsequent rehabilitation and reconstruction stages than their counterparts – Tamil and Sinhalese women – due to their cultural, religious and social background. This paper analyses the impact of the tsunami on Muslim women of the east and the role they played in rebuilding their society. It also looks at the rigid and discriminatory systems and social fabric of this society that negatively impacted the space claimed by these women in the immediate aftermath of this disaster. The case studies in this paper narrate these women's success and painful experiences. It specifically points to the fact that only a few women from this community servived the backlash against their post-tsunami activism while recognizing the fact that these women lack an environment that nurtures and strengthens their newly claimed stature.

This is a great tragedy and a collective punishment of Allah. If you look at the satellite pictures of eastern waves that wiped out our villages and towns you can see that it has the shape of Allah written in Arabic. It wiped out mostly Muslims because they were engaged in 'un-Islamic activity.' (One of the Trustees of Addalaichenai Mosque)

Before December 26/04 the people in the East, indeed in communities throughout the island, had been traumatized by a series of events arising from a variety of sources including militarized violence, economic exclusion, social marginalization, political alienation, domestic and sexual abuse. The tsunami only heightened the effects of this chronic serial traumatization. While it is clear that the impacts of these events have battered all communities, it is also important to recognize that they weave together so tightly that it is futile to try to disentangle them. (Hogan)

Background

The tidal waves of 26 December 2004 ravaged the nations of the Indian Ocean Basin from Indonesia to eastern Africa. The waves killed over 230,000 people and displaced one million. Sri Lanka, an island in the direct path of the tsunami took the brunt of it and two-thirds of its coastline was washed away. According to a government report released on the first anniversary of the disaster (Ministry of Nation Building and Disaster Management) 35,322 people were killed, 21,441 people injured and 516,150 people internally displaced. The estimated economic value of the lost assets is US$900 million; the number of lost livelihoods is 150,000. Ninety-eight thousand houses were damaged, 75% of the fishing fleet was destroyed and 23,449 acres of agricultural land were salinated (von Braunmuhl). The tidal waves struck at a time when Sri Lanka was struggling with a delicate peace process between the Government of Sri Lanka (GOSL) and the Liberation Tigers of Tamil Eelam (LTTE) that had been deadlocked since April 2003, although a truce signed between the GOSL of the time and the LTTE with Norway's facilitation in February 2002 was still holding.

The geographic impact of the tsunami was uneven. The northern and eastern provinces were hit particularly hard, accounting for two-thirds of deaths and almost 60% of the displacement. Women and children were the worst affected by the tsunami. A survey of 53,613 tsunami-affected families indicated that 70% more women than men died. Nevertheless, one in every five tsunami-affected households is now run by women (United Nations Sri Lanka).

According to World Bank reports (World Bank *ADB*; World Bank *Millennium*; World Bank *Sri Lanka*), the eastern districts (where Muslims were hard hit) accounted for 41.1% of the financial needs. The southern and western provinces accounted for 29% and 12.6% respectively. The north, where the Tamils live, accounted for 17.2%.

This small and third minority of the island took more than its share of the tsunami tragedy but faced a raw deal in the post-tsunami reconstruction, especially when compared to how quickly the government took care of the south. The Muslims in the east became the group that was largely under-represented and marginalized in the post-tsunami rehabilitation and reconstruction process.

Introduction – tsunami devastation on Muslims

According to statistics published by the Tamil daily newspaper *Veerakesari* on Monday 24 January 2005, out of the then-estimated total death toll of 30,718 on the island, 12,562 were Muslims. Thus, even though Muslims constitute only 8.9% of Sri Lanka's 20 million people, they accounted for 40.9% of the dead. The overall island-wide figure for the missing was 5815. Out of this, 1980 (34%) were Muslims. Of the 14,998 injured, 7285 (48.5%) were Muslims. Of 85,833 houses which were fully damaged, Muslim houses accounted for 21,751 (25.3%). Out of the 36,616 houses partially damaged, 12,207 (33.3%) belonged to Muslims.

It has been said that disasters, however natural, can be discriminatory and their consequences profoundly gendered. Wherever they strike, they hit pre-existing structures and social conditions that determine how a community will be affected and who will pay the highest price (Oxfam International). This paper will explore the gendered and differential impact of the tsunami on women and men of the Muslim community in the east. Apart from the fact that more Muslim women than men were injured or killed, Muslim women also faced divergent challenges in the immediate aftermath and in the subsequent rehabilitation and reconstruction stages than their counterparts – Tamil and Sinhalese women – due to their cultural, religious and social background.

The specific vulnerabilities and capacities of men and women, as well as the gender/social dynamics of disaster situations are often not obviously visible. In contexts where women and girls have fewer capabilities and resources than men and boys, women's capacity to adapt to natural and human-made disasters such as conflict, earthquakes, and tsunamis, can be compromised. Scholars take the view that such crises can in fact exacerbate existing inequalities between and among women and men and intensify gendered experiences of poverty, gender inequality, vulnerability and resilience to crises. At the same time, disasters can also open up spaces to challenge discriminatory practices and empower women through processes of rebuilding and reconstruction.

Muslim women and killer waves

Ampara, which is the only Muslim majority district in Sri Lanka, was the hardest hit by the tsunami and statistics show 7258 Muslim deaths. If one looks at the death toll of predominantly Muslim villages like Kalmunai, Sainthamaruthu and Ninthavur that got hit worst, the death toll of women outnumbered men and children substantially. For example, in Kalmunai 636 Muslim women died in comparison to 286 men and 204 children (District Secretariat Ampara, Muttur and Batticaloa). In Saithamaruthu, 466 women died while the death counts of men and children were 117 and 182 respectively. In Ninthavur 68 women died, compared to 14 men and 42 children. In Muttur DS division, the worst hit areas were Thakkwa Nakar, Vattam and Habeeb Nakar; the total Muslim death toll was 296, and out of this 184 of them were women. In Batticaloa, Kattankudy was hit hard too, and 112 Muslims died; out of this were 37 women, 50 children and 25 men.

Generally the tsunami took more women's lives than men and children. This tendency of higher fatalities among women has been noted among other communities as well. However, the difference in the death toll between women and men in Muslim areas was particularly marked. It is possible to identify a number of reasons behind the higher death toll of Muslim women.

In Ampara, Muslims live largely along the coastal belt, and most of these coastal villages are densely populated with houses, mainly concrete structures all crammed together. When the tsunami struck most women were in their houses, probably taking care of their children and other family members while the men were away on errands or fishing far out at sea. It is believed that Muslim women were particularly hampered by the clothes they were wearing – loose, long garments with the addition of a shawl as well as their long hair. The clothes and hair appear to have become entangled with trees and fences, entrapping women and eventually drowning them. Some of the respondents also said women were traditionally not taught to nor accustomed to swim or climb trees like the men, and therefore they could not escape the second and third waves even though some survived the first wave, which was much smaller than the subsequent waves.

We were told by men who performed rescue work in the aftermath in the east that young women who survived the first wave, which was mild in comparison to other two waves, but whose clothes were swept away, did not want to get out of the water since they did not have adequate clothes on their bodies. According to a doctor from Ashraaf Memorial Hospital, they had two young women patients who consistently talked about walking out from water without adequate clothes on. One of them underwent serious mental distress and even tried to commit suicide. Later she was treated by a professional psychiatrist.

The other argument that came from women survivors we interviewed is that when the first wave struck women sent their children and men to get to the high ground or away from the coast, but they themselves went back to their houses to grab valuables, especially jewelry, cash, and important documents like title deeds since these have been traditionally in their possession. According to the eye-witnesses and survivors, many lived through the first wave but the second and third were the killer waves, at least in the east.

Practice of Iddah

Widowed Muslim women were perhaps the first of all the ethnic communities to experience the gendered consequences that the tsunami unwittingly gave rise to. According to Muslim law, on the death of her husband a Muslim woman has to observe Iddah. This is a period of four and a half months after a divorce or death, during which a woman may not marry another man. Iddah was intended to ascertain whether the newly divorced/widowed wife is pregnant from her divorced or deceased husband. In Sri Lanka Iddah is marked by strict seclusion of women during this period, as well as other customs such as wearing of white. In a situation of unparalleled disaster where women had not only lost their husbands, but other family members including children as well as their homes, the need to go through Iddah became an additional burden on widowed Muslim women. Although in disaster situations, sometimes traditional cultural/religious practices might be temporarily suspended, this was not the case in relation to Iddah for many Muslim women in the east.

A social activist who went to Kalmunai on the second week after the tsunami had this to say:

> I heard that many women were observing Iddah in Kalmunai with the help of a mosque group and had no access to organized relief distribution. So I collected some money and went to see them, they were all kept in a building that was located by the side of the mosque. I was not granted permission first and the mosque team overseeing the welfare of these women demanded that I give them the cash and they will re-distribute among the widows. I have to fight in great deal and prove that I am a Muslim. Then they asked me to come next day wearing proper Islamic clothes. Next day they had arranged a local woman to take me to this facility to see these women. There were about 40 of them put together in that one open building. Some had infant children, few of them were pregnant and they were all dressed in white thick saris with full-sleeve blouses. It was extremely hot in this overly crowded building and few of them had fever and sore-eyes. Many had lost more than one family member and did not have any access to the outside world. Not even a councilor or a doctor had visited them. They were all given a Qur'an, a prayer mat and some Hadiths books to read. When I asked the mosque team that managed this place whether they can have access to a woman councilor they said reading the Qur'an and praying to god will heal them.

Given that seclusion was mandatory during the period of Iddah, widows were unable to deal with public officials regarding matters of compensation, and therefore were often excluded from initial government and NGO assistance. Those who left the camps to stay at relatives' houses to perform Iddah may have been more affected.

A note from a female INGO officer:

> The Muslim women who have lost their husbands are now in seclusion (four and a half months of mourning period called Iddah) and the worst part is that they are accommodated in someone else's house through arrangements made by the mosque groups. To tell you the truth their current condition is worse than being in a jail. They are kept in dingy corners without ventilation and sunlight and many of them are unable to get even their paperwork done to claim their compensation. As an outsider to this community I was barred from meeting with these women to help their compensation forms properly filled.

Entering the public domain

In the immediate aftermath of the tsunami, Muslim men and women worked shoulder to shoulder performing rescue and relief work including searching for missing people and identifying bodies. Staff at the Ashraaf Memorial Hospital recall women coming into the hospital carrying injured people and helping the overwhelmed hospital staff in numerous different ways. Women also brought cooked meals for people who were engaged in life saving work round the clock for the first couple of days. In a group discussion with NGO and INGO workers, participants recollected how quickly women got together and cooked food for the entire neighborhood. They pointed to the fact that it was local women activists who mobilized volunteers in the camps. Some women's organizations like Akkaraipattu Women's Association, Affected Women's Forum, Suriya Women's Development Centre, Community Trust Fund and Rural Development Foundation quickly mobilized their women's forums and strengthened their activities.

Unlike war-affected Tamil women in the east, the Muslim women had relatively less experience in mobilization in the aftermath of crises and catastrophes. Prior to the tsunami they did not have much work experience or interaction with well-established and resourceful INGOs and NGOs. Only a handful of Muslim women worked in the non-profit sector. Those who had some experience were those who had worked with Muslim internally displaced persons (IDPs) due to the conflict in Kathankudy, Muthur, Kalmunai and Akkaraipattu. These women were the first catalyst group that brought much needed help and knowledge to organize camps, register the affected and seek assistance from various apparatus. Even though mosque groups were active in conducting religious rituals for the dead, helping families recoup the losses through community prayer and helping and feeding the affected who took refuge in the mosques, they did not dominate the immediate relief and rehabilitation, at least for a couple of weeks.

According to some of the women we interviewed, there was considerable space for socially active women who were also affected and who had sought refuge in different temporary shelters to play a leadership role in coordinating relief efforts with individuals and institutions, as well as donors and government officers.

This actually placed many young Muslim women at the forefront of the recruitment list of the INGOs that flocked into the area in the aftermath of the tsunami. Many of these women were recruited by INGOs, particularly those who had already established some link with affected people and community leaders. Women who had never had a regular job found INGO positions with extraordinary salaries and perks based only on their voluntary work within the community. Women who could speak English were paid over Rs 2000 per day just to accompany foreign NGO workers and translate for them.

Chaos created by outsiders and backlash against INGOs and Muslim women working in INGOS and NGOs

In the immediate aftermath, the east (especially Batticaloa and Aampara districts) was inundated with foreign experts who were free to walk into camps and carry out any activities. In certain cases they distributed medicine without approval from the DPDH or local hospitals. Sometime in the latter part of January and beginning of February 2005 there were many complaints of some unauthorized foreign doctors distributing medicine in camps that were located in remote areas of these two districts. In a camp in Akkaraipatu, some locals were able to gather outdated antibiotics and vitamins distributed by these foreign doctors. In some cases the expiry date was October 2004. There were Chinese, Israeli and American doctors who walked into camps on their own and distributed medicine without properly studying the medical history of people. Some of these medicines have caused allergic reactions, and side effects of these medicines are still unknown.

Trauma counseling was another preferred subject of these foreign experts and there were many foreign groups that worked on the psycho-social aspect of tsunami-affected persons in the east in the immediate aftermath. There were two reasons for east to be the favorite target of these foreign experts. Many areas in the badly affected area of the north (Mullaitheevu) were under the control of LTTE and the affected areas in the south were managed by the government, and on the surface looked better developed. For the same reason, Batticlaoa and Amapara were also targeted by many foreign researchers and journalists who went round with their translators collecting appealing stories while compelling the victims to recollect their horrific experiences. There were also many short-lived INGOs which even went to the extent of demarcating the territories in Ampara and Batticaloa and did not want others to work in their areas.

Speaking to a group of affected women in a village in Addalaichenai (Kochchipatti Kiramum) we were told that the third and fourth weeks after the tsunami were very chaotic. Many donors from the West poured in and started establishing their own offices. Addalaichenai is a predominantly Muslim area that is closer to Akkaraipatu, which has long been a tense area due to Muslim–Tamil clashes, and which has always resisted NGO presence in the area. The sudden influx of Western donors was immediately seen as a threat to the community as a whole. On the fourth week, some Canadian doctors went into a temporary shelter (in which Kochchipetti villagers were given refuge away from the sea) and distributed vitamins, since it had many women who were lactating or were pregnant. That evening a group of Muslim youths stormed into the camp, gathered all the vitamins from the women and burnt them. When asked for an explanation it was said that the Westerners were distributing contraceptive pills with the agenda of making Muslim women infertile. A young woman who had assisted in bringing the doctors to this camp challenged the men to replace these pills with proper vitamins if they thought that those were contraceptive pills, but she was then banned from entering the camp. The community organization for which she worked fired her the next day for challenging the mosque's decision. Within two days of this event men started stoning NGO and INGO vehicles that entered Addalaichenai. There was a rumor that a well known Catholic INGO that has been in operation in the East for many years had distributed a bag of dry rations which contained a bible translated into Tamil. Mosque groups mobilized and went around the camps looking for bibles and warning the affected people not to seek any help from any INGOs. The anti-INGO sentiment among men of Addalaichenai spread quickly to Akkaraipattu, Kalmunai and Muttur – predominantly Muslim areas that were hit worst as well. Until the INGOs and mosque groups came to some form of understanding, women in the camps faced extreme difficulties in accessing any assistance, even getting milk powder for their infants.

Women working with INGOs also faced a backlash. The new trend of women becoming highly paid and intermingling with westerners became a huge issue for the eastern mosque groups and men in general.

> On April 2 2006, the Tamil Veerakesari, carried a report on a speech made by TNA MP Mr Ariyanendran at a seminar on 'Tamil Women and Culture' at Tirukkovil. In his speech Mr Ariyanendran stated that he had information about a high rate of abortions in the Eastern Province; he quoted precise figures, 183 for Batticaloa and 163 for Amparai within the past year. He cited the employment of young women in NGOs after the tsunami as being responsible for extra-marital sexual relationships, pornography and the spread of disease and called on all NGO workers to respect their culture.
>
> Some extremist groups picked up on the MP's statement and issued a call for women to cease working in NGOs, through the informal distribution of a leaflet. The leaflet apparently originated in Kalmunai, and bore the name of Affected Women and Women's revolutionary Army of Tamil Eelam (Batti/Amparai). It reiterated the MP's ideas that employment in NGOs would ruin young women's lives and future, and called on young women to leave their jobs by the 15th April 2006. The leaflet also held parents responsible for the actions of their daughter. The Veerakesari of April 7th carried a description of the leaflet and reiterated the demand that women leave their jobs by April 15th and linked this declaration to a Muslim Cultural Group. (Women and Media)

There were many stories of naming and shaming, and personal attacks on women who secured high level jobs with the post-tsunami INGOs. In Ampara, an Italian INGO was warned about employing Muslim women. This INGO was accused of forcing their female employees to take off their headscarves while in the office premises. Our investigation revealed that these women willingly removed their scarf when they underwent residential training, which comprised only women. This INGO constantly received threatening notices from extreme groups and was compelled to hire young Muslim men instead of women. A former staff member of this INGO told us that many Muslim women who worked for this INGO were harassed on the streets on their way to work by an Islamic group, and they were compelled to resign. In fact, many women were forced to sever their connection to NGOs and INGOs. Some of them insisted that they be provided with transport to travel back and forth to work, but it did not work out. Ironically the INGOs which stressed women's rights and equality so much did not hesitate to offer the vacancies to Muslim men when these women gave up their jobs due to such harassments. A former female officer from this INGO said that she could not avoid wondering whether these young men used religion as a means to take away her highly paid and privileged job.

'Mubeena'

Mubeena is working for an organization that focuses on youth development and conflict resolution in the east. When the tsunami hit she used her connection with NGOs and international community to help her community. She particularly focused on helping affected youth. First her fiancé refused to marry her. Her active role within the community was interpreted by the extremists as leading to social ills. A Moulavi, at a Friday prayer speech, accused NGO women of spreading sexually transmitted diseases after accompanying Western men. On that day a youth gang threatened her and told her to quit her job, though she refused. Two days later they pasted posters on the wall of her house accusing her of having sexual relationships with her colleagues. She was able to resist these threats and harassment, because she had the support of her family, especially her father. Today Mubeena is a well respected civil society activist in her hometown, irrespective of the fact that she still continues to receive threatening messages from an extremist group.

In the last 15 years Islamic radicalism has slowly but steadily taken a deep root in the east. There are many groups like Tableeq Jamat, Jamaat-e-Islami, Tawfiq Jaamat, Tharicathul-Muslimeen and so on. In October 2006, followers of Sufi Islam in the town of Kathankudy were attacked and their mosque demolished by mobs incited by orthodox Wahhabi clerics trained in Saudi Arabia. A clear example of the nature of radicalism taking shape in the east can be seen if one carefully observed the sign boards and shop name boards in Kathankudy town. All women portrayed in these sign boards and shop advertisements are either blackened out or their faces and body are covered by an additional layer of black paint which actually makes them look like they are wearing the Burqa. Under influence from the Middle East and as a result of the rise of Islamic fundamentalism globally, more women in the east are wearing the burqa and hijab today than they did in the past. There is clear generational gap with older women tending to wear saris, which they use to cover their heads, while younger women rarely wear the sari in this style, opting instead to wear a head scarf and in some cases even hand gloves.

There is a visible assertion of orthodox Islam within the Muslim community and in the post-tsunami environment; many women who have managed to salvage a well paying NGO/INGO job find such orthodox Islamic practices have been used against their progress. Within two months of the tsunami, many Muslim women who had secured NGO/INGO jobs were constantly harassed. Notices appeared in Muttur, Kattankudi, Akkaraipattu and Kalmunai attacking women NGO/INGO workers. Young men belonging to various groups (in two cases we were told they were threatened by Islamic armed groups) printed hand bills and distributed them after prayers near the mosques.

Some women found that notices came up overnight pasted on the walls of their houses, offices and/or parapet walls by some of these groups. Male family members were warned about the misbehavior of their daughters, sisters or wives. One male member we interviewed in Kathankudi stated that he was warned of his wife's un-Islamic behavior in a public Bayan after Friday prayer. We also interviewed seven such women and their spouses, and two of them were not allowed by their family members to work after this type of public humiliation.

A Muslim female aid worker lamented that while women belonging to other ethnic groups are learning a lot about critical issues that face the community through their work with INGO/NGO programs, Muslim women have not benefited in the same way because of the restrictions on them. Other community women in general in the east have gained a lot and they know how to question and maneuver the power structures around them; unfortunately this has not reached fully to our women. It is true that mosques and our men oppose these programs and gathering of women, but INGOs have conveniently taken this as an excuse.

Despite such harassment and threats some women did persist, and they have been able to overcome the harassment and threats with support of family members and colleagues, and continue their work with NGOs.

'Farzana'

Farzana (33), who works for an NGO that promotes peace and reconciliation, had this to say:

> Although several hand outs were issued about me that I am going behind my foreign colleagues and one day I will be converted to Christianity, I stood up and focused on advancing my career. They even threatened me with death and for many days my mother had to accompany me to the office. I learnt to ignore these and started focusing on educating myself, but my economic situation didn't allow me to continue my higher studies. I then approached several institutions run by the Mosque Federation here. They didn't want to assist me as I am a young divorced woman and working for an NGO. I waited for some time and managed to allocate some money out of my earnings to continue my studies. I have also progressed in my career considerably and have created a place for myself within both the Tamil and Muslim communities. I strongly believe that one day I will become a highly influential person within my society and will be a role model for other women. Most importantly I will definitely give a hand to affected women like me. I want to become a journalist so that I can write about Muslim women's sufferings – we are all collectively punished for simply being women.

A group of professional men we met in Ampara took the view that the tsunami had opened up new opportunities and new ways of thinking. They stated that after tsunami the community as whole has focused on education. Loss of businesses and properties induced youngsters to seek higher education opportunities which benefited women as well. They felt that the women within the community have more space now to pursue higher education and seek employment. According to them young men from their area now prefer their future partners to be employed and to share the economic burden with them. INGO jobs are considered lucrative, yet they stressed that government jobs like teaching and clerical posts are still the most preferred for women since they involve pensions.

They also acknowledge that even though there was resistance at the beginning against women working in NGOs and INGOs, it is nevertheless seen as a positive trend now. They stated that 'before the tsunami there were only a handful of charitable organizations and our women worked for these organizations, but the post tsunami period brought in many western donors and some of the short lived INGOs had more than a rehabilitation agenda which shaken the community.'

Psycho-social counseling

In communities where the traditional gender division of labor still predominates, gender roles will dictate that women become the primary caretakers for those affected by disasters – including children, the injured and sick, and the elderly – substantially increasing their emotional and material work load. As a result post-disaster stress symptoms are often, but not universally, reported more frequently by women than men.

While many people within the Muslim community recognized that the unprecedented nature of the disaster would have an extremely negative impact on the psychological well being of the community, there was little capacity within the Ampara Muslim community to address those impacts. The attitude of religious leaders, who came to dominate reconstruction and rehabilitation in the post-tsunami period, towards psychological stress was to read the Qu'ran and pray. This was of course not sufficient in most cases.

The research team met with a group of women who mobilized through their mosque and went into camps and houses that hosted the affected women in order to help alleviate their pain and suffering. All they could do was say a few consoling words and ask the women to be patient and pray hard. They said that their team included a female doctor as well, but not a gynecologist because although the gynecologist (VOG) in Kalmunai happened to be a woman, she was still a non-Muslim. A young teacher who went with this group told us that after two such trips, she felt that their visits were not contributing in any way towards improving the depression and psychological stress of the affected women. She said, 'I know I have to face the affected children when they get back to school in a few days so I approached a NGO to get some professional advice and they got down a professional councilor who in turn trained 18 of us to deal with these cases. Later I was able to identify two cases that needed clinical treatment and connected them to a psychiatrist in Batticaloa.'

A doctor from Ashraf Memorial Hospital said that after the tsunami many female teachers followed a course in counseling conducted by the South Eastern University. At least 28 Muslim women have completed a one year diploma course in guidance and counseling at the South Eastern University and their contribution really helped in the long run in dealing with issues of trauma. At present, the presence of a number of trained female councilors is a great asset because no one within the community recognized nor knew about post-traumatic stress disorder. The community also did not believe in seeking social or medical treatment for trauma, and the healing did not go beyond religious rituals and payers. Only serious mental health cases were taken to the psychiatrist. He further stated that given the fact that there is a dearth in the country of psycho-social professionals, the tsunami brought this knowledge and training to our teachers, nurses and community mobilizers. This will prove to be useful not just to help people affected by the tsunami, but others in the future as well.

Strengthening of mosque committees

Even while, in the immediate aftermath of the tsunami, both men and women were actively involved in relief work, gradually the relief and rehabilitation came to be formally organized through mosque committees. Later, when more organized and large assistance came, the mosques in respective areas took control of this work. They organized teams consisting of men to oversee various relief efforts and communicate with the state/civil society mechanisms that were put in place. The control of mosques extended even to widows who were observing Iddah; their welfare was also brought under the control of mosques and anyone who wanted to help these women was compelled to go through relief teams comprising only men.

Women in camps particularly felt disadvantaged and experienced many difficulties in fulfilling their basic needs such as water and sanitation, shelter, as well as accessing relief items since they did not have much bargaining power with mosque committees. Among them were widows, pregnant women, lactating mothers with infants and many young girls who got their menses due to panic and stress. They were all pushed to a helpless position and they did not know how to get their special needs fulfilled when it was managed by the mosque and its men. Later, after much advocacy, the Federation of Mosque Committees appointed women volunteers for a short while.

Livelihood concerns

Most of the Muslims who lived in the costal area of Kattankudy and who were hit by the tsunami were displaced from Kichamplam, Olikulam and Sigarum villages, which bordered Tamil villages during ethnic tensions in the 1990s. When they were living in their native villages most of these Muslim women were the main bread winners of their families, and their main livelihoods were weaving mats and making and selling snacks and breakfast. After they moved to Kattankudy they slowly built up their livelihoods from scratch. Palamunai and Punochimunai are two other tsunami-affected villages. Muslim women from these villages were highly entrepreneurial. Their weaving industry was, however, totally dependent on the supply of weaving grass from Tamil women. After the tsunami, due to displacement and relocation they could not restart their weaving as everyone became dependent on NGO assistance. An aid worker told us, 'even though they are resettled back in their areas, their position of not having their own income through their work is not alleviated. They remain dependent and still expect someone to assist them.' According to the Rural Development Officers and the Grama Sevekas in these areas, two factors are responsible for this state of affairs. Generally, livelihood assistance was focused around men and the fishing industry. Furthermore, Muslim women's income generation activities were home-based and were not immediately recognized leading to difficulties in accessing government compensations, subsidized loans or even non-governmental grants. Widows who have recommenced their livelihood activities were nevertheless finding it difficult to market their products without the support of their husbands due to restriction on their mobility and child care responsibilities.

'Fazmina'

Fazmina is 25 years old and got married when she was 18. She refused to marry again since she opted to take care of her daughter, but she needed a male to market the mats that she weaved. Usually this was done by her husband. Fazmina now lives with her mother who lives with her elder daughter after Fazmina's father's death. They both weave mats and Fazmina's brother-in-law sells them, but the money does not go back to these two widowed women. Fazmina worries that her six-year-old daughter will end up weaving mats for her brother-in-law instead of going to school.

There were six widowers who acknowledged that prior to the tsunami their wives made a substantial contribution towards their livelihood/business ventures. Three of them were petty traders and their wives produced the items that were sold in their shops/moving carts. Four of them said that after the death of their wives, they started working for a daily wage and have no idea how to restart their own businesses without the support they had from their wives.

Muslim female-headed households

While it is true that more Muslim men than women were widowed as a result of the tsunami, many women also became widowed adding to the large number of female-headed households in the Ampara District. According to census data there were a total of 27,570 female heads of households in the district prior to the tsunami (Department of Census). According to an aid worker, who works for a well-established INGO that has been present in Batticaloa over the last 10 years, a survey of female heads of the household revealed that around 17.5% of families in the east are headed by women. These statistics, however, are not disaggregated according to ethnicity/or religion, and therefore it is not possible to say how many of these women were/are Muslim women.

The creation of female-headed households is not all war-related. According to Kanchana Ruwanpura's research amongst female heads in the east, female headship also occurs as a result of divorce, abandonment and natural death. Ruwanpura also refers to situations of *de facto* headship, i.e. women being forced to take on headship because the husband is terminally or mentally ill, disabled or is an alcoholic (Ruwanpura).

What the interviews for this study revealed is that while female headed households in the east were targeted for development interventions due to their large numbers even prior to the tsunami, these interventions often did not include Muslim women.

Unlike the Tamil community in the east, prior to the tsunami, Muslim women heading households were not widely acknowledged by NGOs and INGOS. Even long-established INGOs such as Care International and Oxfam officers accepted that prior to the tsunami their statistics on women-headed households in the east did not include Muslim women. There was a general tendency to leave the Muslim community out, partly due to the difficulty in mobilizing them and partly for political reasons. This kind of step-motherly treatment given by INGOs towards the Muslim community has had a major impact on the progress of Muslim women, particularly in the east.

In the east, there have been many micro credit programs that exclusively targeted female heads of households before the tsunami, but such programs did not often include women from the Muslim community. NGOs highlighted that the problem is twofold; that it is difficult to mobilize Muslim women and that, unlike women of the other two communities, it is difficult to get Muslim women to attend meetings, workshops or come for exposure visits. They are mostly restricted to their homes. The other reason is that micro credit programs involve not only recovery of the original amount given as a loan but also 10–15% interest. Paying or receiving interest is prohibited by Islam and these credit schemes did not take root among these women. Since sustainability of these micro credit programs was partially depended on the interest recovery, the NGOs stated that they could not waive it either. It is interesting to note that in 1974 Mohammad Yunus of Bangladesh established Grameen Bank involving mostly Muslim women as his customer base, and to date his bank has lent $4.7 billion to 4.4 million families.

Impact on moveable/immovable assets

Apart from the impact on human life, the impact of the tsunami on property in the area was equally disastrous. Due to the practice of dowry and matrilineal inheritance patterns among the Muslim community in the East, many of the houses destroyed by the tsunami were owned by women. Owners whose houses were damaged or destroyed were entitled to compensation to rebuild their houses. Those who were in the buffer zone declared by the government, however, were forced to relocate. They were also entitled to compensation or a new house built by NGOs/INGOs on behalf of the state.

Of the women that were interviewed for this study, most of them had received compensation to rebuild their houses. We came across only one case where a widowed woman had not obtained compensation for her damaged house as her brother-in-law had obtained what was due to her. She has consulted many lawyers and has been told that she does not have a successful legal case against her brother-in-law. The house was built on her land by her deceased husband who had obtained a joint loan with his brother to build the house. While she was in seclusion (Iddah) in her brother-in-law's house she says that she signed many documents and she believes that one such document has been used to prove that the ownership of the damaged property is with her brother-in-law.

A rapid assessment made by women's groups after the tsunami showed that 60% of land in Batticaloa was owned by women. This is due to the customary laws practiced in the Eastern Province where land ownership went from mother to daughter (Emmanuel). However, when families were relocated, housing allocations were often given to male members irrespective of who owned the destroyed house prior to the tsunami. In many instances, the land titles were given on the basis of the head of household as mentioned in the 'tsunami cards', which were issued by the State for the purpose of distributing relief.

However, we did meet a number of women who had gained ownership of new houses/apartments in Ampara. They acknowledge that at the initial stage they had problems doing their paperwork, but since the land that they lived on with their husbands and children was given to them as dowry it was not a major problem to prove their ownership. We met 18 women who now own a house.

However, it was very disturbing to hear many of them saying that they willingly gave up the ownership of their property to the surviving male family members since they were not comfortable going to the office of the District Secretary, the local politician, INGOs and NGOs to get the necessary paperwork completed and expedite the transfer of ownership. Two sisters from Maruthamunai acknowledged that they tried a couple of times to go into these offices and they found that with men competing so viciously and officers ignoring and harassing them, they opted to put in the name of a male family member as the beneficiary. An elderly woman who gave her ownership to her grandson told us that due to heavy competition and malpractices of the officers she thought her young, politically influential grandson would stand a better chance of getting onto the priority list than her. A few others stated that they feared facing legal consequences since there were so many actors involved in the land reallocation and building process, as well as many political maneuvers and misconduct. For these reasons they preferred their male family members taking the ownership. One woman went to the extent of saying that she completely trusted the men and it was not an issue about which she worried unduly.

Out of the 37 affected Muslim women we spoke to, 22 of them said that they have got some form of housing now. Widows complained that they lost the opportunity to claim for the initial compensation and cash allowance given by the government since they were observing Iddah, but later they were able to secure a house.

Apart from immovable property many women also lost other assets. Many victims complained that they do not have the habit of banking their savings, and most of them invested their money in gold jewelries. The tsunami took away all of it. There was no way of seeking compensation for these women's lost savings.

Remarriage

Losing one's house, land (buffer zone) and savings (jewelry) brought yet another problem to families that had young women. They could not get them married since the families could not afford to give them the promised dowries. Many marriage proposals broke especially because the girl's promised property in the coastal belt became worthless. Many of these young women are still finding it difficult to find marriage partners.

Women who were widowed following the tsunami are also finding it difficult to remarry. Even though Islam promotes remarriage there is general hesitancy to marry young widowed women. As a result, many poor young women and tsunami widows remain single and dependent on their parents or extended family members. Out of 18 young widows interviewed only three were remarried. However, it was emphasized that in the aftermath of the tsunami, since many women died leaving their children and husbands in a destitute condition, the mosque and family members actively promoted remarriage of widowers and many widowers married young unmarried girls.

'Saleema'

Saleema was 16 years old when the tsunami struck Maruthamunai. Her elder sister Haleema and a six-month-old infant died in the disaster. Haleema's husband moved into Saleema's mother's house with the three children who survived. Five months after her sister's death Saleema was stopped from attending school and was forced to marry her brother-in-law, since Saleema's mother thought that by getting her younger daughter married to her son-in-law she could prevent some other outside woman taking over her grandchildren. Now Saleema has two children of her own and also takes care of her sister's three children. During the interview she sobbed and told us that all her classmates have sat advanced level exams with good results.

Generally widowed men preferred to remarry younger women. There were nevertheless some instances where middle-aged women that we interviewed had received a marriage proposal. However, several of them had refused to be married again. There were two reasons that came out clearly during our conversations with them. One was that after the tsunami these single women have accessed some form of employment or income generating avenue, and half of them have even acquired a new home. This economic freedom has given them strength to take care of themselves and their dependents. Their reluctance to get married again also stems from the increase in abuse of alcohol, drugs and violent behavior of men that has been witnessed widely after the tsunami, particularly within the Muslim community. One of the widows we interviewed when talking about finding a compatible partner stated that some men from her camp sold the milk powder and the feeding bottles of their babies to buy alcohol and cigarettes, and they forced their women to beg for food while indulging themselves in various prohibited activities under the guise of being traumatized.

Violence and abuse

A group of affected women we interviewed in Akkaraipattu said that in their camp there was not much sexual abuse since they lived in separate tents or huts, but some women privately spoke of sexual abuse and harassment that they had experienced at the hands of their relatives when they temporarily sought refuge in their relation's houses in the immediate aftermath of tsunami. Most of the widows we met now live with their extended families and they have complained about abuse and exploitation, but none of them wanted it detailed in this report.

An activist from an Ampara-based Muslim women's organization told us how they managed to protect some children (especially girls) from abuse. They had established a

Trust and given scholarships to children who lost one or both parents. One vital condition of accessing this three-year scholarship was continuity of schooling of these affected children. It was distressing for us to find out that, after the devastation, most young girls were stopped from going to school and were forced to take care of the surviving family. This happened to girls who lost their mothers, grandmothers or elder sisters to the tidal waves. Besides, some of the extended family members who adopted these children did not have the financial means to send them to school. In addition, there was a growing concern of incest taking place in camps and crowded houses, and these children did not have a way to communicate even to their close family members because within this society there is a complete denial of the occurrence of such incidents. We were able to relocate two girls who had been sexually abused to an orphanage in Colombo. No legal action was pursued as there was fear about the repercussions of such action.

Conclusion

This paper has sought to highlight some of the differential impact of the tsunami on women and men within the Muslim community in east. The more positive impact of the tsunami appears to be that it opened new spaces for Muslim women to enter the public domain as social/NGO workers. While the threats and harassment meant that many women were discouraged from continuing this work, others who persisted have been rewarded with new roles within the community. Training in counseling has also developed a new cadre of confident Muslim women who can play a role as social workers. Many Tsunami programs are now, however, in the process of leaving the area and the long-term impact of the tsunami on Muslim women's employment, leadership and community activity in the area is to be seen in the future.

The other issue that emerged as part of this research is the dearth of Muslim women taking up critical issues within the community. The few who have overcome many hurdles and backlashes find no support system or progressive leadership to back them.

Note

Field research for this paper was undertaken by a team of three women from Eraur, Muttur and Akkaripattu; for to their safety their names have been omitted. We have also used pseudonyms for the women interviewed herein.

This research was conducted with the help of the Social Scientists Association – Sri Lanka as part of their pamphlet series entitled *Women's Experience of 2004 Tsunami in Sri Lanka*.

References

Department of Census and Statistics. *Ampara District Report*. Ampara: Department of Census and Statistics, 2001. Print.

Emmanuel, Sarala. *Suriya Women's Development Centre, Sri Lanka*. Web. Jul. 2009. <http://www.apwld.org/tsunami_reconstruction.htm>.

Hogan, Paul. *Butterfly Peace Garden Annual Report*. Batticaloa: Butterfly Peace Garden, 2005. Print.

Ministry of Nation Building and Disaster Management. *Building Back Better*. Colombo: Ministry of Nation Building and Disaster Management, 2005. Print.

Oxfam International. *Gender and the Tsunami, Oxfam Briefing Note*. 30 Mar. 2005. Web. Jul. 2009. <http://www.oxfamamerica.org/newsandpublications/publications/briefing_papers/briefing_note.2005-03-30.6547801151/bn_tsunami_gender033005.pdf>.

Ruwanpura, Kanchana. *Matrilineal Communities, Patriarchal Realities: A Feminist Nirvana Uncovered*. Colombo: SSA, 2005. Print.

United Nations Sri Lanka. *Post-Tsunami Recovery and Reconstruction. UN – Contribution to Transition from Relief to Recovery, December 2004 to December 2006*. Colombo: OCHA, 2007. Print.

von Braunmuhl, Claudia et al. *Tsunami – A Study on Disaster Response in Sri Lanka*. Germany: Medico International Bread for the World and Henrich Boll Foundation, 2006. Print.

Women and Media Collective. *Women and Media Collective statement*. Apr. 2006. Web. Aug. 2009. <http://www.wluml.org/english/newsfulltxt.shtml?cmd%5B157%5D=x-157-537121>.

World Bank. *ADB and JBIC, Joint Damage and Needs Assessment*. Colombo: World Bank, 2005.

World Bank. *Attaining the Millennium Development Goals in Sri Lanka*. Colombo: World Bank, 2005.

World Bank. *Sri Lanka Development Forum: The Economy, the Tsunami and Poverty Reduction*. Colombo: World Bank, 2005.

Bending bodies, borders and desires in Bapsi Sidhwa's *Cracking India* and Deepa Mehta's *Earth*

Rani Neutill

Ethnicity, Race and Migration, Yale University, New Haven CT, USA

Deepa Mehta's *Fire* gained much attention, both in India and internationally, as the first film to document a queer relationship between two South Asian women. What has been underexplored in Mehta's feminist trilogy – *Fire, Earth*, and *Water* – is how each film is set upon representing one particular form of violence against women within South Asia. *Fire* deals with the suppression of female desire, *Earth* with the violence against women during the Partition and *Water* with the treatment of widows in Hinduism. Mehta is so firm in documenting these oppressions individually that she is ultimately unable to capture the complexities of what she seeks to represent. This is best illustrated when comparing her second film *Earth* to its original narrative form: Baspsi Sidhwa's semi-autobiographical account of her childhood in Lahore during the Partition, *Cracking India*. Given that Mehta's trilogy documents different forms of women's subjugation, it is no surprise that Sidhwa's novel and the Partition would be an ideal fit for her feminist explorations. However, Mehta does not fully represent women and men's bodies in their different forms of agency the way that Sidhwa's novel does. In this essay I explore how Mehta's film represents the multiple violences against women and men as they are figured in the novel, but ignores the queer identifications and desires that saturate *Cracking India*. While Mehta's *Earth* stresses the violent reality of women's bodies as national metonyms, Sidhwa's *Cracking India* is able to represent both the violent repercussions on women's bodies during the Partition and simultaneously the queer bonds and bodies that emerged during India and Pakistan's creation. Sidhwa's *Cracking India* asks us recognize formations other than the national, through creating a queer liminal space. I argue that Mehta's traditional feminist perspective of representing women's subjugation obscures her ability to represent Sidhwa's novel beyond the heterosexual matrix of nationalist violence. As a result Mehta misses the radical sites of queer and feminist resistance that Sidhwa's narrative offers.

In the very first scene of Deepa Mehta's *Earth* (1998) the camera zooms in on young hands drawing, and slowly tracks back to unveil a little girl coloring a map of India. An adult voiceover (the voice of Shabana Azmi) tells us of the events that are going to follow: 'the arbitrary line of division that the British would draw to carve up India in August, 1947 would scar the subcontinent forever.' The person speaking in the film is an *adult* Lenny Sethi, the narrator of Bapsi Sidhwa's *Cracking India* (1991) from which *Earth* is adapted. *Cracking India,* Sidhwa's third and semi-autobiographical novel, is set in Lahore and narrated through the eyes only of a *young* Lenny, who as a Parsi is a minority and outside of the Muslim-Hindu-Sikh violence of Partition. Young Lenny narrates the division of Punjab as it occurs before her eyes and the multiple forms of violence that are inflicted against the nation's subjects, in particular women. From the onset of the novel Lenny is a strong and willful character afflicted by polio. In *Earth*, by contrast, Lenny does not speak throughout this first sequence. Instead, she breaks a glass. By means of this visual and material metaphor she simulates the breaking of India. By doing so, she suggests the breaking of bodies and the bending of desires that do not fit with what the nation determines is in its 'best interest.' Lenny's silence in the film and the shift from a young Lenny narrating the novel to the camera and an adult voiceover as narrator in the film indicate the kinds of changes that take place in Mehta's translation from novel to screen. It is through these translations and interpretations that we can see how, paradoxically, the breaking apart of India is also a moment at which its newness as a nation was violently asserted, its borders defined, its bodies and their various desires disciplined.

Mehta's *Fire* (1996) gained much attention, both internationally and in India, as the first transnational film to represent an erotic relationship between two South Asian women.[1] What critics of Mehta's feminist trilogy of films – *Fire, Earth*, and *Water* (2005) – have underexplored is how each film is one-dimensionally set on representing *a single* form of violence against women within South Asia. *Fire* deals with the repressive apparatuses of the family and religion that work to suppress same-sex female desires, *Earth* with violence directed at women during Partition and *Water* with the social restrictions imposed on widows in Hinduism during the mid-twentieth century. Mehta is so grounded in documenting such oppressions individually that, though an admirable goal in itself, she is ultimately unable to capture the complexities of what she seeks to represent. Concurrently, one could argue, the *only* thing Mehta desires to portray is violence against South Asian women. The aim of this essay is to explore what the consequences of such an agenda are, which subjects are foreclosed in the making of these narratives, and the resulting effects. I do this through an examination of the differences between Mehta's *Earth* and Sidhwa's *Cracking India*. While in *Earth* there is a valid and important critique of the gendered nature of nationalist violence, Mehta reifies the nation and nationalist structures by giving preference to a heteronormative narration of the breaking of India. Conversely, *Cracking India* both points out the violence of the nation state and deploys a Parsi and therefore perhaps a non-nationalist perspective of sexuality in its representation of Partition.

South Asian feminism and its discontents

The project of State building is invariably a gendered and sexualized phenomenon. The overwhelming number of women raped during the Partition of India is an example of the manner in which the creation of the modern nation state occurs in tandem with the sexual violation of bodies and the organization of desires.[2] Nationalist movements, particularly in the case of South Asia, have conceptualized sexual deviation as important threats to political projects. Nationalism's political goals generally identify non-heteronormative sexualities as politically subversive threats inasmuch as they are figured as challenging the role of reproduction and thus the nation's sanctity and perpetuity. The recovery and study of non-heteronormative sexuality has been a recent movement in South Asian feminism through the work of Gayatri Gopinath (*Impossible Desires*; 'Communal Property'; 'Queerdom'); Paola Bacchetta ('Hindu Nation'); Nivedita Menon (*Sexualities*); Rajesweri Sunder Rajan (*Signposts*); and Kavita Daiya (*Violent Belongings*). In particular, Gopinath and Daiya map South Asian feminism's historical preoccupation with the effects of nationalism on *women*. They examine the ways in which even though South Asian postcolonial feminism has been critical in examining and critiquing the gendered nature through which colonial, anti-colonial and nationalist discourses are produced, it has not been as fervent at examining the 'production of heterosexuality and homosexuality within these discourses' (Gopinath *Impossible Desires* 136). That is, although postcolonial feminism has been crucial in understanding the ways in which nationalism used and abused women, it has not taken into consideration the ways in which the Partition of India became a form of state sanctioned and mandated *heterosexuality*. In this essay I argue that critical examinations of Bapsi Sidhwa's *Cracking India* have overlooked the ways in which the Partition was a process of eradicating multiple and playful forms of desires. In addition, Mehta's filmic adaptation, *Earth*, fails to represent these aspects of the novel and in doing so duplicates the projects of nationalism by denying various forms of sexual identification.

Mehta does not represent women's bodies and their different forms of agency in the ways that Sidhwa's novel does. I look at how the film *Earth* represents the violence against women during the Partition of India as it is figured in the novel, but ignores the multiple queer identifications and desires that are integral to the novel. By *queerness* I mean sexuality that goes beyond the male-female and homo-hetero binaries crucial to the exclusionary reproductive politics of modern nation-states. In comparing the novel and the film, I show that Lenny, the young protagonist of *Cracking India,* as well as other characters, are marked by complex sexual identifications. At the conjunction of non-normative identification, desire, and embodiment, I will show how Mehta's film undermines homosocial play represented in the novel in order to overemphasize the violent use of the female body in the nationalist formation of India and Pakistan. My turn toward *Cracking India* is crucial in exploring how Partition – a violent repercussion and statement of nationalist politics – foreclosed the possibility of non-heteronormative sexual desires. Simultaneously, Mehta's adaptation, in not representing these scenes of desires, does not adequately portray the violence that was the Partition and ultimately enacts a discursive form of violence by denying the multiplicity of sexual desires the novel portrays by ultimately replicating the repressions she seemingly sought to undermine in *Fire*.[3]

Earth denies the multiplicity of desire and thus queerness by solely representing the 'cracking of India' in terms of the symbolic and real use of women in the creation of modern Indian and Pakistani nationalism.[4] In this respect Mehta duplicates the projects of nationalism insofar as she omits the existence of desire that is outside male-female heterosexuality. I look at the multiple sites of queer desire and violence against men *and* women in *Cracking India* order to show how the nation state produces and disciplines *all* forms of sexuality.

This is not an argument about the richness of novels and the paucity of cinema, nor an argument about the authenticity of either the 'original' text versus the adapted; in fact, one might say that both are transnational texts produced by diasporic artists. Hence, before critiquing the ways in which Mehta's film translates Sidhwa's narrative I want to acknowledge a point made by Jigna Desai in her essay 'Homo on the Range: Mobile and Global Sexualities.' Desai argues that Mehta occupies the 'ambivalent position of [being a] diasporic cultural producer who is framed as native informant in the West and who in the postcolonial state must vacillate between national celebrity and contaminated Westerner' (Desai 78). Desai is astute in arguing that Mehta is in an ambivalent position as a transnational filmmaker. Both Mehta and Sidhwa are diasporic subjects and they both create transnational cultural objects, but what they ultimately represent is radically different. Here, both women's ethnic and national identity and audiences must be situated as it lends insight into the differences between the texts.

Sidhwa has lived with other constraints than those of Muslim women in Pakistan depicted in the novel given that she is Parsi. However, one could argue that this difference allows her to critique and document the birth of Pakistan because of her unique outsider position. She also addresses English speaking and reading audiences within Pakistan and in the West as an insider in the sense of being a Pakistani writer, but as an outsider as she is external to the Hindu/Muslim divide. This unique position is different from Mehta who was born into a Hindu family in Amristar and whose family, like many Hindu families, fled there during the Partition. Additionally, Mehta's film is in Hindi and circulates more widely as a result of her medium. Thus, Mehta bears a bigger responsibility in representing the events of Partition. My turn to the biographic here is not to reduce the difference between each narrative to some biographical truth, but to suggest that the politics of ethnicity may play at least some part in shaping each work.

Earth's representation of Partition (and I would argue her trilogy as a whole) constructs 'third world women' as a monolithic object of study, as she positions herself (unwittingly) as a native informant. *Earth* reduces sexuality to violence, and in doing so reifies the colonial notion of the necessity to save 'brown women from brown men.' I believe that particularly because Partition films in India are highly nationalist[5] and therefore heteronormative, in making the first transnational film on the Partition, what critics of the film have called a documentation of India's 'holocaust' (Barenscott), any feminist critique of the Partition must examine the *multiple* borders, bodies and desires that were violently foreclosed in the making of the two nations. *Cracking India* bears the labor of showing desires and sex outside violence that are then subject to the violence of nation building.

The nation determines gender roles and the Partition is a clear example of this. However, it also determines heterosexuality as the firm matrix of kinship. Thus in critiquing the nation (or Partition) postcolonial feminists and even queer theorists end up duplicating what they seek to undermine, which is a gendered and homosexual/heterosexual, and gay/lesbian binary. My essay looks at the moments of queer desire and 'play,' both male and female, and how they exist but are in fact undermined through national upheaval, but must be recognized, and recognized in conjunction in order to move away from strict binaries that delineate heteronormative and pure notions of gendered states. Although Gopinath is correct when she argues that 'diasporas are narrativized through the bonds between men' (5), in order to unveil the heteronormative discourses of the nation and the diaspora we need to look at both sites of gay/lesbian desire. They are not of threat to one another and they are not mutually exclusive. In fact in not combining analysis that takes into account both we reinforce a binary that perpetuates an identity politics that separates gays and lesbians, or same sex desire on the part of men and women, from mobilizing politically. *Cracking India* and Mehta's filmic adaptation are ripe sites for exploring these omissions, experiences, identifications and desires precisely because they are about the Partition – a representation of the violence of national and nationalist upheaval.

The bending of *Earth*

Mehta's translation of *Cracking India* into *Earth* not only flattens out the narrative by sticking to a predisposed Western narrative of the subjugation of Women in the Third World and the postcolonial feminist articulation of representing the ways in which nationalist movements particularly used women, it actually empties many of the characters of their actual *character*. Lenny and Papoo (the sweeper's daughter) are both filled with the willfulness and rebellious curiosity of being children and are not given this role within Mehta's filmic scope. Even Lenny's ayah, mentioned by name only once in the novel as Shanta, is a far more nuanced character. Certain female characters such as Slavesister,

Godmother, and Hamida, and certain instances like the mother's use of petrol to help move women across the border, even while she is being abused and cheated on by her husband, are completely absent in *Earth*. It is clear that certain omissions are necessary to translate a novel to the screen due to the difference between written as opposed to visual and auditory media – each possesses its own codes, conventions, constraints and possibilities. Nevertheless, it is important to ask, what is left out, added, and why?

In her book *Violent Belongings: Partition, Gender, and National Culture in Postcolonial India*, Daiya criticizes Mehta's adaptation. She writes:

> ... in her translation of the novel into film, Mehta fails to destabilize conventional South Asian rhetoric around ethnicity, gender and identity.... The filmic plot itself elides the complex relationships and betrayals that Lenny slowly apprehends in her family.... *Earth* thus sanitizes the multiple stories of betrayal, violence and love in the novel, creating an idyllic, romantic, pre-Partition picture of middle class domestic bliss. (Daiya 56)

Daiya's assessment of the film as a sanitized portrayal of the novel is correct. However, to argue that there is any 'pre-Partition' narrative in *Cracking India* is problematic.[6] This is even more the case in *Earth* as the first half of the novel is absent from the filmic diegesis. In accordance with Daiya there is a 'heteronormative ideological rhetoric [in] Earth' (Daiya 59). Here, I also suggest that in replacing the narration of the film with an adult flashback instead of the child narration in the novel, and ignoring the first half of Sidhwa's text, Mehta negates the very complexity of the historic moment she adapts to the screen – the Partition – and the subject whom she portrays as victim – women.

Daiya argues that the novel has 'two threads,' one which is 'the domestic, everyday conflicts and concerns that mark Lenny's coming of age; the second the Partition' (Daiya 58). To say that the novel has 'two threads' denies the multiple stories and desires that are *interlinked* and ultimately foreclosed by the eventual nation building. The 'domestic middle class bliss' and the secular and working class alliances that are represented in *Earth* are used to overemphasize the violence of the Partition. In *Cracking India* the domestic arena is fraught with Lenny's 'father's extra-marital affair, her mother's protests, and the bruises on her mother's body from domestic abuse' (Daiya 59). The failure of *Earth* is tracing Shanta's narrative, who was victim to nationalist ideologies of 'fallen' women as socially dead,[7] while in the novel she is sent to Amritsar. In *Earth* the closing scene is a shot of Bapsi Sidhwa in Lahore's Queen's Garden. Shabana Azmi's adult voice over states: 'I never set eyes on her again.'

The novel is provocatively ambiguous on the subject of heterosexuality and the agency of women that Mehta fails to represent in the film. The 'one thread' of Lenny's 'coming of age' is in tandem with the birth of two nations, and Lenny's coming of age turns out to be the disciplining of her play as a child which includes an eroticized relationship to Shanta and the exclusion of play between men that is mandated with the birth of independent India and Pakistan.

Queer play

It is not as though the predetermined identities of 'lesbian' or 'homosexual' are played out in *Cracking India*. In fact, by using a child narrator who is going through puberty the novel is able to resound with sexualities beyond any fixed binary of straight or gay. The novel presents the possibility of sexual desire as fluid and outside the predetermined desires of a heterosexual matrix. In 'Outing Heternormativity: Nation, Citizen, Feminist Disruptions,' Nivedita Menon problematizes the use of the terms gay, homosexual or lesbian as it relates to South Asia. Menon describes the complexities of labeling sexuality and a distinction that has been made between 'men who have sex with men' (MSM)[8] and 'gay.' Citing the work of Shivananda Khan (the founder of Naz Foundation International) she notes that he makes this particular distinction in order to talk about men who he interviewed who did not refer to themselves or identify as gay, who are attracted to women, but have sex with men. These men according to Khan see this act as 'having fun, or *masti* (meaning fun in Hindi)' (Menon 16). The term *masti* adequately describes the 'fun' between men that happens in *Cracking India* – or what I am calling 'queer play.'

There are three scenes that mark the evolution from queer play/*masti* to the violence of the Partition, and they all involve Hari the gardener. Hari is described as a sexually ambiguous figure. Lenny compares Gandhi to Hari: 'He looks like Hari, our gardener.'[9] This comparison between Gandhi and Hari places Hari in a liminal gender space, as she describes Gandhi in an almost gender queer way ascribing to him a 'hypnotic and dynamic femininity' (Sidhwa 96).[10] The likening of Gandhi to Hari happens after we are given a glimpse of the playfulness that the servant men of Lenny's house have in relationship to Hari's body. In this first scene Sidhwa describes the non-violent, queer play among men:

> They are after the gardener's dhoti.... We approach the servant's yard and, sure enough, see the ragged scuffle around Hari.... Yousaf the odd-job man, Greek profiled, curly haired, towers mischieviously over Hari.... Papoo, the sweepers daughter, who comes galloping and whooping from the servant's courtyard, an infant wobbling dangerously on her hip, and brandishing a long broom. Her wide, bold mouth flashing a handsome smile she plunges herself... and the broom into the scuffle. Yousaf has a grip on Hari's hand – which is hanging on to the knot at his waist. Yousaf casually shakes and pulls the hand trying to loosen its hold on the loincloth, and Hari's slight, taut body rocks back and forth... Hari is having a hard time fending off the cook's hand... and also coping with Moti's sly attacks, and Papoo's tickling broom. The washerman... has also joined the melee. Hari plays the jester – and he and I and they know he will not be hurt or denuded. His dhoti might come apart partially – perhaps expose a flash of black buttock to spice the sport – but this happens only rarely. (Sidhwa 53–54)

Such public display of communal sex involves the presence of an infant, a young girl with a 'tickling broom' and group of groping servant men. The washer-man, the cook, the odd-job man – all domestic servants – want a shot at taking off the gardener's clothes. Men transgress into the feminine – the garden as the site of nature/reproduction, and the domestic as the interior feminine space of the nation. As men occupy 'feminine' roles, Papoo and her metaphorical penis thrust themselves into the 'scuffle.' This passage destroys any notion of the woman as merely biologically by entangling her into male bodies and beyond her essential identity. The playfulness here is obvious, just as is the gender reversals and homosocial recreation. This is a moment of 'jest,' and 'melee,' i.e. *masti* in the truest sense. Hari's body is eroticized and desired, and the fact that Hari 'will not be denuded' contradicts the eventual violence of being denuded. The desirableness of Hari's body is in marked contrast to the next scene in which the men attempt, and are successful, at removing his dhoti:

> Again they're after Hari's dhoti. But instead of the light quick patter of bare feet there is the harsh scrape and drag of leather on frozen earth. It doesn't seem quite right to toy with a man's dhoti when it is so cold. It is a summer sport....
>
> Someone pulls off his shawl and it is trampled underfoot. Hands stretch and pull down his unraveling mauve lady's cardigan (Mother's hand-me-down) and rip off his shirt. His dhoti is hanging in ragged edges and suddenly it's off!
>
> Like a withered tree frozen in a winter landscape Hari stands isolated in the bleak center of our violence: prickly with goose bumps, sooty genitals on display. (Sidhwa 125–126)

The gradual transition from how the domestic servant-men treat Hari in the novel shows an evolution from 'light quick' play to castration and mirrors male bodies being disciplined through the creation of two nations. Once the political rears its ugly head, Hari, who would never have been hurt, who is played with as a 'summer sport,' is reduced to a winter spectacle of 'sooty genitals.' The winter/Partition moves into a time where Lenny knows surely that 'one man's religion is another man's poison' (Sidhwa 125), and the men's relationship to Hari and his body illustrate this shift. Papoo is absent from this second sequence, indicating that as the nation and its religious identifications constitute themselves, gendered bodies are regulated in ways that were previously unseen, much in the same way that religion becomes the means by which otherness is verified. The final scene involves Hari's corporeality, wherein he has become Himat Ali, a Muslim. He is no longer wearing a dhoti; he is now dressed in a shalwar:

> 'Where is Hari the gardener?' someone from the back shouts.
> 'Hari-the-gardener has become Himat Ali!' says Imam Din . . .
> 'Let's make sure,' a man says hitching up his lungi, his swaggering gait bent on mischief.
> 'Undo your shalwar, Himat Ali. Let's see if you are a proper Muslim.' (Sidhwa 192)

The men ask to see Hari's newly circumcised penis. Unlike the previous two scenes the interest in his penis is apparently purely religious. There is no actual move to expose him. In the shift to the violence of the Partition, Hari to Himat Ali, the men are satisfied in not touching him, and ask him to recite the *Kalma* in order to prove his faith. Addressing the violence against men during Partition, Diaya writes of this particular scene: 'Hari's conversion probably constitutes the humiliating, symbolic emasculation of Hindu men for the mob, as well as legitimizes his presence in the new nation-state Pakistan' (Diaya 69). While this is partially accurate, Daiya misses Hari's 'emasculated' body in the second scene when they remove his dhoti. What is far more arresting is that upon the birth of Pakistan they are not interested in seeing the physical proof of his conversion to Islam. Unlike the earlier scenes, where there is a relationship to tactility, a touching among men, when Hari becomes Himat Ali we find that the disciplining of his subjectivity has moved to the linguistic, to his ability to recite the *Kalma*. His body, which had previously been the site of play and desire, is no longer important. In fact, Hari's naked body may even be threatening, possibly a reminder of his erotic and playful arousal.

The move from body to language indicates a shift from the phallus as a desiring signifier, a site of *masti*, to a religious mark and thus a fetish. For Freud, the fetish is a substitution, a way to disavow and avow the mother's lack of a penis (Freud 214–219). In this sense circumcision becomes a fetish, a way to disavow desire through the substitution of a religious mark, but since the fetish is always also an avowal, the fact that the men turn toward the linguistic and not visual proof of Hari's conversion is telling. It is as though Sidhwa is saying, 'yes the Partition regulated bodies and desires, but the desires are still there.' Additionally, through this shift from desire to religious mark, Sidhwa is showing us how both men and women were subject to the violence of Partition, that both male and female bodies were cut and violated, as right after this scene Shanta is taken by the gang of men and raped. The cutting of Shanta is metaphorically relayed when Sidhwa writes that as the men take her away, 'her mouth [is] slack and piteously gaping, her disheveled hair flying into her kidnappers' faces, staring at us as if she wanted to leave behind her wide-open mouth and terrified eyes' (Sidhwa 195).

In *Earth*, the initial two scenes or 'play' around Hari the gardener are absent. In fact, in her translation of Hari's conversion from print to screen, Mehta writes *in* the denuding of

Himat Ali. By writing in Hari's transformation from Hari the Hindu to Himat Ali the Muslim, Mehta represents the violence men experienced during the Partition. In *Earth* the order of demanding Hari recite the *Kalma* and unveiling him is reversed. The man who demands to see the proof of Hari's circumcision gets his wish. We see two faceless men pull his shalwar pants down. There is a shot of his buttocks and then the camera turns to the Muslim man looking at his newly circumcised penis as he exclaims, 'Great!' The camera turns to show Imam Din shielding an emasculated and terrified Himat Ali looking down at the ground. The Muslim man exclaims, 'The barber did a great job on his penis!' The shot of Himat Ali's buttocks is one of castration, not fetishism. What the Muslim man is peering at is a signification of Hari's conversion to Himat Ali, but as viewers we are only given a glimpse of his buttocks and we feel embarrassed for him. In the Mehta's filmic narration there is no 'slight and taut' desirable Hari the gardener, only the 'humiliating, symbolic emasculation of [a] Hindu [man] for the mob.' Hari's provocation of sexual desire, his signification of the queer play among men, is lost on the screen, as is the everyday play that existed among men that is destroyed when Pakistan and India are borne as two independent and supposedly sovereign nations.

'Will the earth bleed?'

This question – 'will the earth bleed?' (Sidhwa 124) – is one that Lenny asks her readers. Lenny's question is nuanced as it refers not only to the actual division of India that she witnesses but the relationship between all the bleeding subjects of the nation that is to be divided, and in particular her own physical relationship to the 'earth' that is otherwise known as the nation.

Upon hearing the idea that the British are the cause for her illness, Lenny feels for the first time a connection to Indian politics:

> 'The goddamn English!' I think... 'They gave us polio!' And not-withstanding the compatible and sanguine nature of my relationship with my disease, I feel it is my first personal involvement with Indian politics... (Sidhwa 26)

It is the compatibility of her body and the nation that gives Lenny her first nationalist sentiment. The use of the word 'sanguine' is provocative. It refers not only to her body but to blood, the blood that ties her to her body as diseased and her desire for Indian independence. It is by all means true that the novel represents the upheavals of the nation as they are played out on the bodies of women.[11] However, the novel simultaneously portrays how Partition comes to destroy the multiple identifications and desires that come from being a child for Lenny. The 'sanguine' relationship that Lenny has to the nation is absent from Mehta's *Earth*. Instead of connecting the spread of polio to the British the film instead declares, 'there was no syphilis in India until the British came.' To take away Lenny's first sentiment to national politics is just one indication of how displaced her character will be on screen from the earlier portrayal in the novel. Sidhwa's Lenny is a charismatic and observant little girl. The film takes this playful child and turns her into a passive observer, devoid of the complex set of burgeoning desires of the literary figure.

The bleeding that Lenny speaks of could arguably be read as the bleeding that will soon come to be part of the embodiment of her womanhood as the novel goes on to detail both the psychical and sexual maturation of young Lenny. Lenny's sexual maturation is described not as a simple progression into heterosexual desire but a complex relationship to sexuality. Desires and identifications that can be seen throughout the first half of the novel are quieted through the loud, piercing and violent upheaval of national politics.

One could argue that understandings of heterosexuality are cultivated through both the enforcement of cultural taboos and the prescription of limited familial sexual identifications. Both such enforcements and prescriptions seek to perpetually repeat and conserve themselves and thereby a nationalist family model defined by what desires and whose can be inside the family and those that must not. In the case of Partition, Sidhwa shows us that it is the nation who usurps the role of the parents and takes on the structures of kinship normally defined by the family. The nation becomes the family and as it does this, it is a far more disciplining form of kinship organizing. It breaks the bodies of women and men and the earth – makes them *bleed* – in order to protect and serve what it deems the natural and to render phobic so-called abnormal desire, desire that I think of simply as abnormal with respect to the dominant norm. The nation relies on women and children to uphold kinship structures. As Lenny becomes more aware of her body's connection to the national body, certain desires are sequestered; ones that could have been cultivated by young Lenny especially are impossible to know. The specters of violence of the nation make it impossible to read what Lenny could have been – meaning, familial structures could have produced Lenny as a normative heterosexual child but the national injunction, the Partition, makes it such that her body and her femininity are over-determined by the historical upheaval that she is subject to. However, we are given glimpses of Lenny's sexuality possessed by desires beyond those the nation considers normative or proper.

Lenny's look

The chronology of sexuality and its representation through women is a key motif throughout the novel. First and foremost, as the narrator of all the subjects and happenings in the novel Lenny is a voyeur and her voyeurism comes to function much like a form of scopophilia, particularly as it relates to the bodies of women. Lenny's voyeuristic relationship to Shanta renders Lenny's growing realization of her own sexuality, but it also functions as a pleasurable relation to that which she gazes upon, which is in marked contrast to her actual sexual play of 'doctor' with her cousin.

Sidhwa underscores Lenny's movement into puberty by heightening the sexual violence of the Partition. The fact of sexual violation is something that becomes ever pervasive in her world through her relationship to both her ayahs – Shanta and Hamida (the ayah who replaces Shanta is from a refugee camp of 'fallen women'). Lenny states that through the doings of Shanta she learns of 'human needs, frailties, cruelties and joys' (Sidhwa 29). Although it is similarly through Shanta, Hamida and the other working class subjects in the novel that Lenny learns and actually sees in graphic detail the horrific events of Punjab's Partition, she is no stranger to war: 'I was born with an awareness of the war: and I recall the dim, faraway fear of bombs that tinged with bitterness my mother's milk. No wonder I was a colicky baby' (Sidhwa 40).

Lenny slowly learns the meaning of sexuality through Shanta. The sexuality that Lenny learns may be couched in heterosexual terms, but through identification with the male gaze that finds Shanta to be the pleasurable *object-to-be-looked-at* (what Laura Mulvey calls a *to-be-looked-at-ness*) (Mulvey 19), Lenny in turn finds pleasure in looking at Shanta:

> The covetous glances Ayah draws educate me. Up and down they look at her . . . . And as if her looks were not stunning enough, she has a rolling bouncy walk that agitates the globules of her buttocks under her cheap colorful saris and the half spheres beneath her short sari blouses. (Sidhwa 12)

In this scene the gaze that educates Lenny is that of the men whose glances tell her where to look. After identifying with the male gaze, Lenny becomes a scopophilic voyeur;

she is placed in the narrative position of looking as her eyes watch the bounciness of Shanta's walk which 'agitate the globules of her buttocks,' and she derives pleasure from watching Shanta's movements. Lenny's voyeurism is not limited to Shanta; we find her frequently looking at women's bodies: 'I... view... the smooth, plump spheres of young women who hide their faces in their veils and bare their bodies' (Sidhwa 60).

In Mehta's *Earth* we are given a visual image of this commentary, but within this visual scheme Lenny's pleasure and voyeuristic scopophilic gaze is absent. Lenny's scopophilia might have been heightened in *Earth* because of film's greater visual potential, but unfortunately, it is not. As Lenny joins Shanta and her admirers at the community park, Shanta's sari falls from her shoulders, exposing her chest which silences the men around her. In contrast to the novel, where Lenny identifies with the gaze of the men and in turn becomes the one to gaze upon Shanta's beautiful and voluptuous body, viewers identify with the men in the film.

In *Earth*, Shanta smiles and the men around her smile back in giddy lust. Ice-Candy-Man (Amir Khan and Shanta's rapist) comes on screen to recite a poem and offers Lenny a *kulfi* Popsicle. Shanta also engages in the act of consumption, taking seeds and nuts from one of the men in the circle that has formed around her. Shanta's sari falls from her shoulder, partially revealing her breasts, and Lenny, in an overly child-like way, continues to eat her Popsicle. The next frame is a close up of Ice-Candy-Man's face, as the sight of Shanta's breasts arouses him, which is different from the next close-up of Masseur (Shanta's eventual lover) who gazes upon the object of his desire, before the camera shifts from Masseur to show a close-up of Ice-Candy-Man again. The camera's move between the two men and their shared, knowing look zooms back to Shanta, who is suddenly aware of her exposure and covers herself up.

Within this sutured scene Lenny is absent and so does not share in Masseur and Ice-Candy-Man's covetous glances. Consequently, she does not identify with the men, her gaze is missing and her pleasure in looking at Shanta is overshadowed by our identification with the men and their gaze. Mehta's filmic representation mimics a very classical model of Hollywood cinema that is famously written about by Laura Mulvey in her path-breaking article, 'Visual Pleasure and Narrative Cinema.' Mulvey writes:

> The scopophilic instinct (pleasure in looking at another person as an erotic object) and, in contradistinction, ego libido (forming identification processes) act as formations, mechanisms, which mould [traditional cinema's] formal attributes. The actual image of woman as (passive) raw material for the (active) gaze of a man takes the argument a step further into the content and structure of representation, adding a further layer of ideological significance demanded by the patriarchal order in its favorite cinematic form – illusionist narrative film. (Mulvey 25)

Mulvey's feminist project is to unveil a contradiction within the scope of traditional narrative film. For Mulvey, to represent woman as icon and object is a threatening thing as it produces castration anxiety. By overemphasizing the females' *to-be-looked-at-ness* calls attention to her very being as a woman, and therefore her difference in the sexual order of things – it calls up her lack of penis. In *Earth*, one could argue that Shanta's ultimate rape, disappearance and the lack of any other strong or even overly present on-screen female character eradicates such an anxiety.

In one of the most violent representations of the Partition in *Earth*, we see Masseur, Ice-Candy-Man, Lenny and Shanta on the roof of a home, watching the violence of Partition erupt below them. A Muslim man, surrounded by a cheering Hindu mob, is ripped apart by two jeeps. The final shot of his mutilated body is his limp foot. We then see a group of Muslim men disguised as firefighters using petrol instead of water to set a Hindu enclave of Lahore aflame. Right after these scenes of violence, Ice-Candy-Man asks Shanta to marry him. Lenny is hidden in Shanta's lap, frightened after witnessing these horrific acts. Shanta shakes her head saying no in response to Ice-Candy-Man's proposal. The camera zooms in to show a full shot of Lenny's face. She is crying and states, 'I'll marry you Ice-Candy-Man.' In contrast, in the novel, when Masseur, not Ice-Candy-Man asks Shanta to marry him, Lenny reacts violently: 'Don't you dare marry him.... Don't leave me... I will never let another ayah touch me' (Sidhwa 168). The particularity of Lenny's desire for Shanta is expressed here, not a desire for Ice-Candy-Man.

Within the narrative scale of the novel, Lenny's look, voice, and presence is a threatening vehicle to the normative sexual and gendered order of things. Although Lenny may be a voyeur in the sense of being a witness in *Earth*, the only time she is an actual voyeur of sex is when she gazes through a window to watch Shanta and Masseur make love. There is a close up of Lenny's face that indicates her looking at the couple. Her gaze is immediately interrupted as we see her look up to find a close up of Ice-Candy-Man looking through a window across the room. The camera turns to Ice-Candy-Man as he looks and walks away to light a cigarette and cry, the camera framed on him and his actions. If we are to identify with anyone in this sequence it is Ice-Candy-Man, or even Lenny's identification with him, perhaps even enough to feel empathy for him to forgive or at least understand what happens next – his rape of Shanta. Throughout the novel Lenny is the voyeur of everything. In the film she is not. She is practically eclipsed by the camera.

Lenny's liaisons

The heterosexual counterpart and play for young Lenny in *Cracking India* comes in the form of her relationship with her cousin. In contrast to *Earth*, in which Lenny's main sexual identification and attraction is for Ice-Candy-Man, Lenny learns about heterosexual desire through the play with her cousin. Her first kiss, for instance, is with her cousin:

> I feel Cousin's wet, puckered mouth on my bunched-up lips. I know I am supposed to feel a thrill, so I muster up a little thrill. The thrill comes and goes.... The Kissing scenes in films go on much longer.... Kissing I'm convinced is overrated. (Sidhwa 153)

Here, Lenny's relationship to heterosexual desire is ambivalent. It is something she is 'supposed to feel,' something that feels 'overrated.' Such ambivalence towards the opposite sex does not end with her first kiss. Her first sexual encounter is with Cousin as well:

> His genitals have grown since I last examined them three years ago.... 'Feel it,' offers Cousin.... 'I have become a honeycomb,' he says. 'Lick me here, and see what happens.' I lick the tip gingerly. Nothing. No honey. 'You've got to suck out the honey.' Cousin arches his back and maneuvers his penis to my mouth. 'Suck it yourself!' I say, standing up. (Sidhwa 172)

The powerful rejection of Cousin's penis is felt in this passage, but as the novel proceeds we find Lenny growing into an 'appropriate' heterosexual woman. However, her heterosexual desires are still marked by complex identifications and longings.

After the violence of national division and Shanta's rape and disappearance, Lenny claims to be 'in love' with every man she lays eyes on. Her attraction to these men is in part learned through the 'rapture Masseur aroused in Ayah' (Sidhwa 230). Although her attraction to men is widespread, her only real encounters continue to be with Cousin. Cousin attempts to woo Lenny's affections and in the process aggravates Lenny. Lenny delivers 'a compromise,'

> A finely delineated covenant: I will keep an open mind and let bygones be bygones, and Cousin will stop wooing me and wait a couple of years before touching my breasts again. We

> shall see how I feel about it then. In the meantime Cousin sensibly sets about becoming indispensible. Knowing the way to my heart, he scurries about trying to find the whereabouts of Ayah. (Sidhwa 245)

Though the proof of Lenny's heterosexual inklings are there, everything seems to be intimately connected to Shanta/Ayah, including the 'way to [Lenny's] heart.' Lenny's interactions with Cousin make heterosexuality less about actual desire and more about a form of forgiveness and an ambivalent possible future.

Cousin eventually finds Shanta. Upon seeing Shanta for the first time since her abduction, Lenny calls her 'achingly lovely' (Sidhwa 273). The novel indicates that Lenny 'properly' chooses men as her choice of desired object, and her being in puberty could be called a liminal state in regards to sexuality, a stage of development to becoming a heterosexual woman. However, the spectacle of the Partition, the nation's disciplining of its subjects, creates an ambiguity around what are one's own desires and what is learned. This is seen in the progression of how the working class men in the novel relate to Hari's body. Additionally, Lenny's use of the word 'achingly' to describe Shanta, even after she has determined herself to be desiring of men, connotes an active desire for Shanta, a desire that was previously only seen through her voyeuristic relation to her, and beyond her childhood gaze and play. In her essay 'Border Work, Border Trouble: Postcolonial Feminism and the Ayah in Bapsi Sidhwa's *Cracking India*,' Ambreen Hai writes:

> [Ayah] becomes the "subject" of Lenny's story, the object lesson of her own (bisexual) adolescence... Ayah is for Lenny simultaneously both [an] intensely desired self and other; she embodies a desirable adult femaleness that Lenny herself both ardently desires and desires to be.... It is perhaps Lenny's desire for this body for which this body will later be punished, and Lenny's desire subsumed by accusations of male violation. (Hai 396–397)

At first glance it appears that Lenny's double desire for and to be Shanta is relegated to her pre-pubescent self. However, the fact that Lenny calls out her desire, her aching for Shanta, after Lenny's 'maturation' into heterosexuality, and Shanta's rape, illustrates that Lenny's desire is not 'subsumed by accusations of male violation.' In fact, Lenny's desire for Shanta persists beyond her violation and, like Ice-Candy-Man, despite it.

Liminal, transnational, national

Cracking India illustrates how the fluidity of childhood desires, the play of homosocial bonds within male friendships, and the play of being a child are interrupted by the nation. As many South Asian postcolonial feminists have so incisively shown, the nation has a direct and violent relationship to its gendered subjects. Sidhwa's novel illuminates how it also regulates desires to the point of diminishing any 'play' of a child or adult. Through Mehta's adaptation, the richness and importance of this play, and the eventual foreclosure of it, does not survive. Such a move and omission is continuous with the way Partition has been narrated by postcolonial feminists and critics. The novel has elements of queerness as it challenges the sole emphasis on the gendered nature of violence during Partition. This emphasis on gender is intolerant of questions of desires that are disciplined and corralled in the interest of nation building. In doing so, as does Mehta's *Earth*, it problematically reinforces the logics of nation building, the very thing it deems violent. In theory both the novel and film could mitigate against the dominant ideology of the production of heteronormativity. In the case of *Cracking India* and *Earth*, the novel does and the film abjures. As a result, the film misreads the novel's purpose – not to let us forget that these sexualities exist, even if they are rendered aberrant.

Cracking India shows how multiple bodies and desires are repressed, violated, mutilated, and written upon in the process of nation building and border-making. In her seminal feminist text *Borderlands*, Gloria Anzaldua describes the border as '*una herida abierta* where the Third World grates against the first and bleeds' (Anzaldua 3). Although the Partition is not the collision of the Third World against the First in the sense that Anzaldua describes, it was the opening of a wound. For Anzaldua the liminal, transitive space of the borderland is a fertile one, where *los atravesados* live, 'the squint-eyed, the perverse, the queer, the troublesome, the mongrel, the mulato, the half-breed, the half-dead; in short, those who cross over, pass over, or go through the confines of the "normal"' (Anzaldua 3). *Cracking India* presents the liminal, queer, 'in between' space(s) that Anzaldua speaks of, a space that the nation cannot accommodate. Ironically, as a transnational film, with all the purpose and fruitfulness of this status, *Earth*'s failure to represent these spaces reproduces the normative ideology of the nation.

In conclusion, I return to the importance of understanding the transnational and diasporic in order to appreciate what may have played a part in the radically different shape of each text beyond a question of individual form. Sidhwa published *Cracking India* in 1991, before the expansion of Hindu nationalism, a growth in the number of communal riots, and before the 1992 conflict around Ayodhya. In 1998, the time of *Earth's* release, the rise of Hindu nationalism showed its full presence when Atal Behari Vajpayee, leader of the Bharatiya Janata Party (BJP), became India's prime minster and two months later five nuclear bombs were tested in the desert of Pokhran, Rajasthan. Since the nation is intimately connected to its subjects, including the diaspora, the diaspora was also nationalized. It is not surprising then that *Cracking India,* written prior to this rise of Hindu nationalism, and *Earth,* produced during the waves of these tensions, are very different representations (despite the fact that one is adapted from the other) of the Partition. Precisely because the diaspora itself became a site of nationalism, Mehta is able to play the role of native informant reproducing the logics of nationalism through the production of heteronormative discourses and the representation of a Hindu woman (Shanta) as *the* site of violation in the making of Pakistan. Sidhwa, writing from the liminal perspective of an outsider, before the rise of vehement Hindu nationalist politics, shows us the complex sites of sexual identifications and desires beyond the reproductive, repressive and violent rational of the nation.

Acknowledgements

I would like to thank the Whitney and Betty MacMillan Center for International Studies and the Program in Ethnicity Race and Migration at Yale University for support instrumental in the creation of this project. I want to thank my fellow Postdoctoral Associates Lourdes Gutierrez Najera and Raymond Orr. I would particularly like to thank Jigna Desai, Avak Hastratian, Gita Rajan and Nguyen Tan Hoang for their invaluable intellectual and editorial advice while configuring the arguments of this essay.

Notes

1. Mehta's first film in the trilogy, *Fire*, brought the question of non-heteronormative sexuality to the forefront of Indian politics. When the film was distributed in 1998, the Hindu Right vehemently attacked it. The assault brought out public demonstrations against homophobia and censorship to the cities of Mumbai and Delhi in numbers that were previously unseen in India. Menon, in her essay, 'Outing Heteronormativity: Nation, Citizen, Feminist Disruptions,' argues that, although there have always been private and public forms of what she terms 'counter-heteronormative' sexual practices and identities in South Asia, the 1990s were

a defining moment in terms of the creation of a visible queer movement, and the reaction to *Fire* is indicative of this moment in Indian political movements (Menon 16). Paola Bacchetta has argued that to label the 1990s as a definitive moment for the emergence of a queer movement in India ignores the existence of queer identities that stretch back before the 'U.S.'s existence as a settler colony itself' (Bacchetta 111), and the 2000 publication of *Same Sex Love in India* by historians Ruth Vanita and Saleem Kidwai documents queer love back to the Vedic texts. I agree that to claim the 1990s as any 'origin' of queer social movements in South Asian is deeply problematic. What interests me, however, is not a question about the beginnings of a social movement. Although Mehta's *Fire* provides the first transnational representation of a queer relationship and the ensuing backlash against her film spawned political mobilizations around queerness, she fails in *Earth*, to narrate the complexities of subjectivity and desires that Sidhwa's novel documents, and instead turns the history of the Partition of Punjab into a tale of politics, class, heterosexual romance and betrayal.

2. What is most striking about the Partition is the fact that over 100,000 women were raped and mutilated. As post-colonial feminists Ritu Menon and Kamla Bhasin describe the distinctiveness of the different atrocities: 'Stripping; parading naked; mutilating and disfiguring; tattooing or branding the breasts and genitalia with triumphal slogans; amputating breasts; knifing open the womb; raping, of course; killing fetuses' (43).
3. As Gita Rajan has argued in her essay, 'Pliant & Compliant: Colonial Indian Art and Postcolonial Cinema,' in *Fire* Mehta creates a lesbian coupling only as a default or choice by necessity option after the failed heterosexual relations for each woman with her husband (one is ascetic and the other is a lothario – without critiquing their deliberate withholding of sexual engagement). Consequently, homosexual desire or, rather, homosexuality itself in *Fire* follow a default trajectory that Deepa Mehta charts to stay within the safe limits of nostalgic, diasporic audience acceptance and conservative nationalist depictions of feminine subjectivity (Rajan 48–69).
4. South Asian feminist criticism and postcolonial criticism of nationalism explain how the female body has been constructed as the symbol of purity and distinctiveness in nationalist discourses. This critical illumination spans through the work of political and colonial historians, most notably Kumkum Sangari and Sudesh Vaid, Partha Chatterjee, Lata Mani, literary critics such as Sangeeta Ray, and the invaluable work of feminists Kumari Jayawardena and Malathi de Alwis, Ritu Menon and Kamla Bhasin, sociologist and feminist Veena Das and the oral histories of women, children and *dalits* documented by Urvashi Butalia in her book *The Other Side of Silence: Voices from the Partition of India*. Partha Chatterjee's groundbreaking work *The Nations and its Fragment: Colonial and Postcolonial Histories* details the category of woman as critical to Indian nationalist rhetoric. Chatterjee shows how the discovery of tradition was a nationalist strategy used to create an identity distinct from that of the colonial powers through distinct gendered and dichotomized categories of inside/spiritual/female and outside/material/male. While, as I have mentioned earlier, Gopinath points to the omission of the production of discourses of heterosexuality and homosexuality within nationalist rhetoric and state violence in the above body of work, Daiya ponders, '[w]hat happens to men's roles, male bodies, and conceptions of masculinity in the discursive articulation of nationalism in the postcolonial sphere?' She further argues that we need to 'complicate the question of "gender" and "woman" to offer a fuller account of the gendering of nationalism… [and] that it is imperative to examine the construction of both masculinity and femininity together in the articulation of cultural and national belonging in public and political discourse' (Daiya 41).
5. *Bombay, Hey Ram, Pinja, Gadar Ek Prem Katha* to name a few.
6. The rumblings of the 'cracking of India' happen as early as page 22 where the question of governing a nation is compared to the governing of a household. Lenny's mother states: 'And you all want Pakistan! How will you govern a country when you don't know what goes on in your own house!' (Sidhwa 22).
7. Ritu Menon, Kamla Bhashin, Urvashi Butalia, Veena Das, Kavita Daiya.
8. The acronym MSM is not South Asia specific. In the US the neutral social science term used in HIV/AIDS education is MSM as well.
9. Sidhwa 95.

10. There has been much work on Gandhi's sexuality, most notably Sudhir Kakar's *Intimate Relations: Exploring Indian Sexuality* in which Kakar provides a psychoanalytic reading of Ghandi's sexuality, arguing that his obsession with celibacy and self-discipline were a means to desexualize women and feminize himself.
11. As argued by Sangeeta Ray, Ambreen Hai, Kamran Rastegar, and Mehta's *Earth* to name just a few.

References

Anzaldua, Gloria. *Borderlands: La Frontera*. San Francisco, CA: Aunt Lute Book Company, 1987. Print.

Bacchetta, Paola. "Rescaling Transnational 'Queerdom': Lesbian and 'Lesbian' Identitary-Positionalities in Delhi in the 1980's." *Sexualities*. Ed. Nivedita Menon. New Delhi: Kali for Women, 2007. 103–27. Print.

Bacchetta, Paola. "Communal Property/Sexual Property: On Representations of Muslim Women in Hindu Nationalist Discourse." *Forging Identities: Gender Communities and the State*. Ed. Zoya Hassan. New Delhi: Kali for Women, 1994. 188–225. Print.

Bacchetta, Paola. "When the Hindu Nation Exiles its Queers." *Social Text* 61 (1999): 141–66. Print.

Butalia, Urvashi. *The Other Side of Silence: Voices from the Partition of India*. Durham, NC: Duke UP, 2000. Print.

Chatterjee, Partha. *The Nations and its Fragment: Colonial and Postcolonial Histories*. Princeton, NJ: Princeton UP, 1993. Print.

Daiya, Kavita. *Violent Belongings: Partition, Gender, and National Culture in Postcolonial India*. Philadelphia: Temple UP, 2008. Print.

Desai, Jigna. "Homo on the Range: Mobile and Global Sexualities." *Social Text* 73.20.4 (2002): 78. Print.

Gopinath, Gayatri. *Impossible Desires: Queer Diasporas and South Asian Popular Cultures*. Durham and London: Duke UP, 2005. Print.

Hai, Ambreen. "Border Work, Border Trouble: Postcolonial Feminism and the Ayah in Bapsi Sidhwa's *Cracking India*." *MFS Modern Fiction Studies* 46.2 (2000): 396–7. Print.

Kakar, Sudhir. *Intimate Relations: Exploring Indian Sexuality*. Chicago, IL: U of Chicago P, 1990. Print.

Menon, Nivedita. "Outing Heteronormativity: Nation, Citizen, Feminist Disruptions." *Sexualities*. Ed. Nivedita Menon. New Delhi: Kali for Women, 2007. 16. Print.

Menon, Nivedita, ed. *Sexualities*. New Delhi: Kali for Women, 2007. Print.

Menon, Ritu, and Kamla Bhasin. *Borders and Boundaries: Women in India's Partition*. New Brunswick, NJ: Rutgers UP, 1998. Print.

Mulvey, Laura. *Visual and Other Pleasures*. Bloomington: Indiana University Press, 1989. Print.

Rajan, Gita. "Pliant & Compliant: Colonial Indian Art and Postcolonial Cinema." *Women: A Cultural Review* 13.1 (2002): 48–69. Print.

Rajan, Rajeswari Sunder, ed. *Signposts: Gender Issues in Post-Independence India*. New Brunswick, NJ: Rutgers UP, 2001. Print.

Sidhwa, Bapsi. *Cracking India: A Novel*. Minneapolis, MN: Milkweed Editions, 1991. Print.

Vanita, Ruth, and Saleem Kidwai. *Same Sex Love in India*. New York: Saint Martin's Press, 2000. Print.

Eat, pray, love, mimic: Female citizenship and otherness

R. Diyah Larasati

Theatre Arts and Dance, University of Minnesota, Minneapolis, USA

Looking at Asia and the Asian Diaspora as a geopolitical post-colonial space, this paper aims to examine the role of travel and tourism as a sign of modernity and how it influenced and reconstruct the use of existing spatial gender categorization in cultural practices. Through the understanding of tradition as a fluid bodily knowledge in contemporary cultural political economics, this paper questions the intervention and innovation of the female bodies in Asian global tourism and indigenous Diaspora subjects within globalization. Based on the novel *Eat, Pray, Love*, by Elizabeth Gilbert, to mediate the analysis of the effect on space in cultural modernity, in the construction of otherness, which provokes the understanding of other culture as 'non-modern' yet reiterating tourism as one of the possible mechanism to mediate this encounter in bringing the 'un-modern' cultural practices to the world of modernity. This paper seeks to discuss the invisibility and visibility of female bodies in tourism space and cultural imagination by using specific examples of various events mentioned in the book that convey contradictory memories and values to local citizens and, in the meanwhile, the space and events are re-appropriated again for the purpose of globalized concern.

In this paper, I chart quests for otherness by uncovering how difference was constructed using colonial ideologies and how it is now perpetuated in another form though discourses of globalization that rest on technicalities of modernization and patterns of cultural consumption (Said 34). Yet, because the processes of othering are always already occluded, the choices to inhabit social spaces are fragile and elusive for those who are othered. By examining one travel narrative from today's globalized moment of modernity, I trace and show how contemporary techniques are but a mirroring of an older, colonial enterprise. However, what happens when the 'other,' mobile and displaced within contemporary global migration, encounters and confronts the colonial archive and the circulating neocolonial text imaging her self, body, and home? This vulnerability of the othered self is seen in the biased self defense mechanism in non-familiar spatial forms, which are dramatized when encountering the traveling or moving body via the memories of the traveler. That is to say, I will explore how Elizabeth Gilbert's best-selling novel, *Eat, Pray, Love* (2006) retraces the same path that Tome Pires charted in *The Suma Oriental* in the sixteenth century to exoticize *my home*. This resonance has a visceral effect on the body, *my female body*, in that it makes the familiar unfamiliar, and forces a problematic engagement with this new unfamiliar.

The discourse of travel in this paper requires us to follow that gaze and look at the non-familiar. This angle of the gaze presents the strangeness and the distance of the referent from the traveler. Travel was mostly created to fulfill the blank spot within the nation and mark the situated self through difference. I view this travel, then, as a strategy to be in another territory, be it a part of the colonial memory that reproduces ethnography or in today's mode as a way to fulfill this emptiness in the frame of politics of pleasure and leisure. In colonial time, travel was initiated from the economically and technologically superior heart of empire to former colonized sites where traditional values were preserved, which, in turn, were romanticized by the imperial traveler (Spivak 97). Therefore, to recapture those differences within a self or a nation requires being identified and categorized as other in one's own homeland. I analyze the construction of traditional values, bodies, and spatial imaginary in colonized places or in a new imperialist term, the 'traditional undeveloped world.'

I. Ethnography: Gazing at the object of travel

On Thursday evening, at the end of April 2009, my body is covered in sweat, as I begin to imagine a *below-the-equator temperature*, even though it is quite cold outside. A small camera is positioned in front of me, and a very serious interviewer is asking me many questions. He, a smart man, uses a Lacanian style of inquiry because he is trained as a psychoanalyst. I remind myself of how Freudian psychology teaches me *not* respond to him. I feel the force of not being 'too' emotional, leaving the present moment, so I will not be categorized as a dramatic reactionary 'third world' woman.

In confessing this, I purposely redefine this past event to avoid the self-implication and framing as a victim. I also withdraw from the geopolitical spatiality of emotional longing, as I do not want to fall into the discourse of Post Traumatic Stress Disorder – associated with the past violence of Indonesia. I am aware of not mixing or conveying fear and its communication, and the memory and the telling of memories of violence as, right now, I must play this position of an expert rather than a victim. I am aware not to fall in to what Elaine Scarry calls 'Distributing the Pain' (177). I am aware.

It is Minneapolis. I knew I made many wrong English translations, but these are layers of consciousness in representing a moment, an embodiment of witnessing while at the same time analyzing the plight of children left behind from the massacres between 1965–1966 in Indonesia. The interview on camera is recapturing my childhood memories, and I confess. The interviewer is referring to the Cold War and women in Indonesia, the fiasco years, the complicated international involvement and the internal power of the Indonesian militaristic style government. I also play a script or 'noise' that has been around: the question of the betrayal, the feminist who always says that she has to cross borders.

One and half hours later, he, the interviewer, puts down his recording machine and turns off the camera. He says: 'let's talk to Elizabeth Gilbert, the winning writer of the *New York Times*, 2006, the best seller, who in her memoir also talks about Indonesia, the place that you are referring too, she [Gilbert] has many connections, and I [the interviewer] will speak to her [Elizabeth Gilbert].' I begin to feel the weight of regret.

Across the hall, a student runs to me; she too wants to talk about the *New York Times* best-selling novel, *Eat, Pray, Love*. 'It is about Indonesia and India,' she continues, 'It is about women, so you should check it out!' I am anxious, searching for the connections between these events or the possibility of a shared reference. Is there one?

Eager to seek those connections, I prepare myself for the contradictory, as I am familiar with scholarship production like the old version of anthropological link. In the same way, I am familiar too with the popular travel notes, as a foreigner encountering a fantasized landscape such as the one famously introduced to us by Gustave Flaubert (Karayani 42).

As a dancer, I begin consciously placing my body – where I embrace and detach from location – at the center of my inquiries of these narratives. I find the rhythm, the dances, the bodies and the undulating stories. I start using many examples from previous works: novel, film, scholarship, and choreography of dance. Soon, my discomfort starts to rise as these previous works always create different layers to my imaginations of *my home*, the more familiar reference of belonging (Ong 5). To take a risk, as my diasporic location grants me, I must acknowledge the differences of the agendas in the popular novel. I allow myself to look at it – the novel that later is announced as a memoir.

Underscoring the unfamiliarity further, the television announces that there is a new film production of *Eat, Pray, Love.* I fear popular imagination becoming a historical construction of a discovery of self against the other, of a journey into exotic lands to make it real, and told still in imperialist mood of the whitened voice through media. It clarifies my shadow of hesitant resistance, building upon my mistrust. I once again am forced to become a reader of this translation from my own language to something that I must consume.

Julia Roberts, together with the Hollywood machinery (the movie is to be directed by Ryan Murphy and produced by Brad Pitt), is cinematically clarifying what has been done by Gilbert to give it a more striking impact. Translations and transpositions of my home into what is consumed as popular culture. I have lost and lose again my home and my access to it. It became and becomes the imaginative place fulfilling the capitalist version of the popular global landscape. I compare.

II. Academy: Extricating the body from discourse

I reach for the archive where, according to the prominent methodology of knowing, I am supposed to locate the picture of *my home* from the old colonial report. I am lost. I see the puzzles of strangeness that those old archives created. I opened them all, and I must confess, I did not feel I knew those places. I, in the middle of the colonial report and of the popular form, locate *my home* and I wonder how to reclaim it. I am lost.

In the writing of my analysis here, I locate the travels, which produced the colonial memory of Indonesia. Nevertheless, they are now repeated and represented through the new wave of popular travel. The idea of otherness that existed, guarded by imperial discourse, is appropriated by many others, and developed into a fossilized zone – my home. This has created a mysterious space, a blue shade of comfort for travelers. Looking at the colonial text, *The Suma Oriental* (Pires 89–90), and *Eat, Pray, Love* by Gilbert, I begin to imagine the space that those writers created. In fact, looking at the resemblance of the contradictions, I tremble at these travelling reports that recapture the dismay we felt when exposed to colonial memory. That mediation only changes names; now it is called an encounter within globalized modernity. This latest affront is a film starring Julia Roberts as the white American writer who travelled to Asia. She feeds off a mesmerizing Indian religion and encounters an Indonesian medicine man to fill the blank smudge of loneliness. Being present in the 'Orient' of the global South allows her to transcend and reconfigure identity based on her choice.

I attempt to re-historize and criticize the production of a Western imaginary for this construction of otherness that swallows up differences. She, my other, understands this travel experience as being anthropologically unique, but simultaneously detaches it as a complicated implication of identity. This is done by conquering, owning, and reproducing some of my cultural imaginary as her discovery. *It means translating herself into the familiar and myself into the unfamiliar.* (I recall the Middle Eastern practice of Belly dancing and the feminist defense of it as a 'resistive practice,' while at the same time rejecting other Middle Eastern practices associated with Islam.) This is a strategy to transmit power and excitement in an encounter for the purpose of reverse psychology.

Tomé Pires, not a notable figure before his travels, garnered the position of Portuguese ambassador to China through his experience and knowledge of Asia. A tradesman and an apothecary before his journey to India, Malacca and China, Pires, by the power of the representative of the Crown of Portugal, traded his knowledge of Asia for a title and honor. His treatise was the first global report writing about Southeast Asia from the Portuguese point of view. This displays not only the blurring of many cultures and nations into the ambiguous idea of the East on the part of the Portuguese, but also how *knowledge* of the East in this colonial context equaled power and opportunity. As his account of Asiatic culture became fact, it was in reality a cultural translation fraught with biases that has colored the colonial enterprise for three centuries at least.

In *Eat, Pray, Love*, the images of India and Indonesia are but pale comparisons to Italy, and serve the need of the traveler's agenda of self-discovery. The writer, a New York woman shaken by her divorce, begins a journey to recover from loss. Although her book begins with an extended stay in Italy (food and architecture) as an ideal place for such a purpose, I should like to focus on the sections on India and Indonesia.

I open to the part about India, where she expresses longing for an imaginary Ashram life. She even allows herself to scrub the floor. She wants to transform *herself* into a 'mystical' girl who 'performs menial tasks as a way to achieve a constant meditative state' (Gilbert 190). In her mind, this searching for God is a sign of the attainment of true otherness. Yet, we grew up familiar with this kind of work, which in Bali (and India) is required as daily duty for women, avoidable only when menstruating because then the female body is considered spiritually unclean. I now remember with wry humor that many of us as young girls claimed to have three menstruation cycles a month in order to avoid this monotonous task which, for Gilbert's hero, is spiritually lifting. The Ashram, as the meditation place in *Eat, Pray, Love* is an alternate, deliberately circumscribed spatial reality. After she gets her wish to do such menial labor, and transforms into the 'mystical' figure, the situation changes. She writes:

> The next morning I was down on my knees in the temple, scrubbing the marble floor again, emanating (I imagined) a holy radiance of silence, when an Indian teenage boy come for me with a message–that I need to report to the Seva office immediately.... Due to the special request from management, I was no longer to be a part of the floor scrubbing team. They had a new position in mind for me at the Ashram. And the title of my new job was – if you will kindly dig this – 'key Hostess'. (Gilbert 193)

III. Situating the other discursively

In fact, such instances of white privilege are not new. We recall many other examples like the colonial travels of Rolf de Mare, the Swedish member of the royal family, who received access from the Dutch Crown to collect Indonesian arts and present images of the now familiar female dancing body. I recall also 'Matahari,' the Dutch civil servant's wife who, mesmerized by the Balinese and Javanese landscape, reconstructed herself as a Javanese princess and later became a dancer for militarized high society in Paris. *Eat, Pray, Love* and the Matahari narrative discursively put into play stereotypes of oriental, dancing female bodies anchored in the Dutch East Indies, and provide us with evidence of the reconstruction of identity. This imagined identity, I argue, is invented through translation in different locations, and keeps proliferating because it is repeatedly reproduced (granted in newer versions) through the distribution of modern and current popular globalized culture seen in the depictions made for mass media (see Matahari in the Indiana Jones television series; Larasati 151). Therefore, through the eyes of the Western traveler from the sixteenth century, continuing through WWI, and via the lens of globalized media today, the portrayal of the Eastern dancing body is homogenized and stereotyped in this type of travel narrative (Savigliano).

I continue reading this modern 'feminist' memoir, looking anxiously for the reference related to the question by my interviewer. On page 238, my eyes open: '100,000 corpses choked the beautiful rivers of Bali when the killing spree was over.' I allow myself to hope, remembering her menial labor meant to signal a rise in her spiritual consciousness; I wonder if she will not submit to the 'consciousness raising' labor involved in uncovering the larger narrative that lies behind this new information about carnage. No, she writes: 'Wait– why did I come to Bali again? To search for the balance between worldly pleasure and spiritual devotion, right? Is this indeed, the right setting for such a search?' (Gilbert 238).

I step back; the 'worldly pleasure' reference shocks me. I want to beg her to look around and honor the women who serve and host her in Bali. They make possible her spiritual luxuries. Women who make the temple beautiful; their hands create the offerings, and manage the household. I wonder if she found the time to converse with them, as she often spoke only of the men – Mario, Yudi, Richard, Felipe, and the Medicine man, Mr Ketut Liyer – why not the women? Had she initiated a more intimate connection to the women surrounding her, she might have understood the complex relationship between the lives of those who serve tourists like her, and the deaths of those who floated in the river. Surprisingly, the female narrator of *Eat, Pray, Love* functions as the distanced witness. The female bodies that become the uncounted encounters – in their lack of movement – make the 'balanced' space fragile, and her writing relegates the 'other' women in India and Indonesia to the position of marginal characters.

Gilbert focuses on the Medicine Man, who teaches her central actor about 'God.' She also speaks about Mario, a Balinese man who loves all things Italian, the reference to which evokes the earlier journey into Europe and indicates Italy's role as marker of Indonesian cosmopolitanism. She maps these markers onto the landscape of Bali as the narrative of her own spiritual journey. (There was already prominent dancer with the name of I [read: e] Mario in the 1930 East Indies of the Dutch era.) In the end, I find it very difficult to recognize *home* as it is described in her writing, even though I recognize her tropes and I am very familiar with her story.

Soon the worlds of the Ashram and Bali grow very small. The Bayung River filled with corpses and flowing through Bali disappears. This same river appears in Margaret Mead's (174) famous anthropological work dotted with many naked breasts. Since the river narrative is part of many local healing practices as well as the colonial and 'modern artist's' obsession to capture erotic, naked bodies bathing or 'releasing nature,' I am surprised at its passing reference in Gilbert. She moves away from Tomé Pires' colonial portrayals:

> it is not a lie that they are so preposterous that they kill themselves with a kris if anything displeases them, and they sometimes kill their husbands; and it is a custom in Java for a woman to be searched before she goes to her husband, because they carry secret krises – traditional weapon – ... (Pires 199)

Similarly, in Luís de Matos' *Imagens do Oriente no século XVI*, women are shown bathing and honoring God, and a widow is seen buried for the passionate love. Such images dominated the representation of Indian women, as well. Gilbert's narrative moves away from this Oriental fascination instead focusing its globalized feminism on spiritualism and cosmopolitanism within Orientalism.

I take a risk in comparing these different historical moments (sixteenth century and the twenty-first century) in order to establish a link between Orientalist productions of knowledge by imperial and global writers, who incessantly circulate clichéd stereotypes as the ground for knowing Asia. Audiences too accepted this *simulacrum* (Baudrillard 153) as truth, i.e. the circulation of images that are reproduced with varying degrees of resemblance to the first stereotypes. The representation of Eastern bodies fashioned during wartime still continues through a postmodern/global space (tourism) in historical reportage, art, novels, and films. The mimicry now is performed by the Euro-American body of Julia Roberts who continues the fantasy of the East. Since this misrepresentation or better yet, this unruliness is carried out by the dominant body, the new body becomes the signifier of otherness.

In this context, Tomé Pires' colonial report, Portuguese paintings depicting Asian peoples published in *Imagens do Oriente no século XVI* (de Matos), and Elizabeth Gilbert's travel narrative culminate in Julia Roberts' retelling of India and Indonesia. Such a simulacrum splashed over time and across continents interchanges the invisibility and the visibility of the female body through spatial appropriation. Those re-appropriations of the female body are fantasized in a popular form as a site of travel and tourism, which are a form of cultural translation. This cultural translation bridges universal mind and body experiences, ultimately defacing the original. From an economic point of view, the travel trajectories of the Euro-American devalue the Asian body.

I close the book. I feel Gilbert's popularized version of 'my home' pushes back the voice of the dead bodies whose chanting calls me to dance and rewrite the narrative of the river. I must work harder to remap the landscape that she 'discovered,' passing by the corpses floating in the Balinese river for the Brazilian cocktail in her spirituality of expatriate life. I recoil at that which creates balance within Gilbert's feminist world – the feminine longing and desire for the colored masculine otherness of Felipe, Mario and David along with the guided meditating mantra of the medicine men.

Rather, I listen for the mantras of the unbalanced voices emanating from my ancestors' bodies that have been relegated to the margins of many writings. I know that the massive publicity machinery of Gilbert and Hollywood will repeat again the disappearance of the corpses. Furthermore, the labor of the women who provide Gilbert's grand tourist hospitality is invisible; this invisibility makes possible a longing for a privileged and glamorous spiritualized loneliness. I move my body to reclaim and rebuild the space where I stand to honor the river and allow the water to flow and fertilize the rice, which my family continues to eat. We cannot escape as those corpses live in our houses, singing the noise that provides fire to light the branches, revealing other feminine dancing bodies who answer our mantras with their own.

We are not the mystical Ashram girl and temple keeper whose silence forgets the dead. We will dance resistively reencountering the rapidly circulating images produced by a predatory feminism that travels through and consumes the 'home' in Asia.

We dance, not toward the allure of the masculine, but in the fertile land along the river encircling it, so that it may never again be filled with the corpses.

Acknowledgement

The author thanks Jigna Desai for the conversation and João Pedro the archive adventure.

References

Baudrillard, Jean. *Seduction: Cultural Text*. New York: Palgrave Macmillan, 1991. Print.

de Matos, Luís, comp. *Imagens do Oriente no século XVI. Reprodução do codics portuguôs da Biblioteca Casanatense*. Lisbon: IN-CM, 1985. Print.

Gilbert, Elizabeth. *Eat, Pray, Love: One Woman's Search for Everything Across Italy, India and Indonesia*. New York: Penguin, 2007. Print.

Karayanni, Stavros Stavrou. *Dancing Fear and Desire Race, Sexuality, and Imperial Politics in Middle Eastern Dance (CS)*. New York: Wilfrid Laurier UP, 2004. Print.

Larasati, Diyah. *Migration and Regulation to the Female Dancing Body: Southeast Asian Bodies in Global Circulation*. Chicago: Illinois Press, 2007. Print.

Mead, Margaret. *Letters from the Field, 1925–1975*. New York: Perennial, 2001. Print.

Ong, Aihwa. *Buddha Is Hiding Refugees, Citizenship, the New America (Public Anthropology, 5)*. New York: University of California, 2003. Print.

Pires, Tomé. *The Suma Oriental of Tome Pires Works and The Book of Francisco Rodrigues. Vol. I/II*. London: Hakluyt Society, 1944. Print.

Said, Edward W. *Culture and Imperialism*. New York: Vintage, 1994. Print.

Savigliano, Marta. *Tango and the Political Economy of Passion from Exoticism to Decolonization (Institutional Structures of Feeling)*. New York: Westview, 1994. Print.

Scarry, Elaine. *The Body in Pain: The Making and Unmaking of the World*. New York: Oxford UP, 1985. Print.

Spivak, Gayatri C. *Other Asias*. Malden, MA: Blackwell, 2008. Print.

Grassroots texts: Ethnographic ruptures and transnational feminist imaginaries

Piya Chatterjee

Department of Women and Gender Studies, Scripps College, Claremont, CA.

> "**Trans-**, trânz-, trâns-, pfx. across, beyond.———Also tran-, tra-. [L. trāns, across, beyond.]" (Geddie, 1167)

> "**Translate**, trâns-, trânz-,træns-, trrænz-lāt', v.t. to remove to another place: to remove to heaven, especially without death; to enrapture: to render into another language: to express in another artistic medium: to interpret, put in plainer terms, explain: to transfer from one office (esp. eccelesiastical) to another : to transform: to renovate, make new from old.———v.i. to practice translation: to admit of translation———adj. **Tran-slā'table.**——n. **translā'tion**, the act of translating: removal to another place, see, &c.: rendering into another language: a version: the working up of new things from old materials: change of place (distinguished from rotation): the automatic re-transmission of a telegraphic message."(Geddie, 1167)

> "**Translation** n., conversion, paraphrase, version, transformation, change, rendition." (Microsoft Word 200 Thesarus, U.S. version)

> "The traditionally desired invisible translation of the original text misreads, replaces and displaces the text—erases it, in fact. But an opaque translation, drawing attention to its own presence in the text, foregrounds the difference between original and reproduction. This is a self-reflexive translation, a thick translation, drawing attention to its own presence and the ideological nature of translation as a colonizing act." (Karamcheti, 193).

Introduction: Tangles and Provocations

Sometimes, I confess, when I am asked to write about the "transnational feminist" implications of my work around Indian tea plantation women's lives, I get mired in a dense thicket of anxieties and questions. How could my ethnographic work located in the hinterlands of eastern India be "transnational"—apart from my own bi-national, diasporic subjectivity and movement? And how can I make legible the feminist commitments and lessons I learn from this space when the primary discussions about the "transnational" and "feminism" appear to be rather firmly located in – or aimed towards the – imperial centers of the North? Almost immediately, I recognize the limiting – but also productive aspects – of these questions, as much as I understand that they gesture to thick, knotty tangles which will be hard to smooth out and braid neatly.

First, as Chandra Mohanty and others have argued, the presumption that a feminist ethnography of tea plantations is a local "case study" which does not impact broader "global" theory is problematic – especially if one implicitly assumed that truly "global" theories are produced first in imperial centers (Mohanty 333–358). The "local" ethnographic case informs "global" theory, at best. Surely, a critical and plural understanding of "transnationalities" break across these epistemic assumptions and binary inequalities. The plantation case is, for example, already global, formed in specific sites by historical transnational processes.

Second, despite de-centering interventions, some might still posit that hegemonic constructions of the "transnational" continues to rest on such an enduring axes of reference – North to South, and vice versa. The imperial vectors of knowledge formation are difficult to dislodge. In that case, feminist ethnographies which seek to wrench the "transnational" away from this bi-lateral trajectory can suggest knowledges that are "otherwise" constituted, otherwise "centered."

Third, there is the presumption that 'feminist' sensibilities that emerge from these local places (out there in the peripheries of the so-called Third World) are not so relevant to the question of difference and power in the feminist preoccupations of the so-called First World. Postcolonial and antiracist feminist scholarship, produced in the past three decades, has certainly revealed these geopolitics of difference and power in the study of women, gender and sexualities, here/there/here. Many feminist scholars/activists have persuasively argued about the "third" in the "first", and for additional critical scrutiny on displacement and poverty in its many forms, mobile, across borders – in the North as much as the South.

This destabilization has helped to produce "transnational feminisms" as a powerful catch-all rubric within which many kinds of feminisms can be grouped. While these destabilizations do highlight multilateral engagements between women, the geopolitical binaries of imperial knowledge circuits still informs transnational projects in enduring ways. As an anthropologist who writes from places which don't have an immediate relevance to this imperial geography, I am concerned with how transnational feminist projects, based and produced in the United States might still obscure these implicit stances of "relevance" and significance.

Why does it matter at all – politically and ethically – to offer stories about plantation women if I choose not to fit them into a South-to-North axes? What if the lack of proximity to Northern preoccupations continue to render such analysis as merely one more entry into the old encyclopaedia of difference that is really still an index for distant strangeness made somewhat familiar? Such provocations open up a rather large Pandora's Box. This is a box that might be stuffed with ethnographic curiosities. They gesture to provisional explorations. They beg grounding.

In this essay, I explore these difficult knots by sharing, with humility and care, some grassroots lessons that I learned from the tensions and fissures of fieldwork in tea plantation country.[1] These are lessons that destabilize. They only begin to explore the big provocations I have set up. The braid I will weave will still have many knots, still remain messy – though that is perhaps the point: producing text through ethnographic methods is a snarly and messy business.

In staging the plantation, and presenting these ethnographic ruptures, I use "translation" as a tool with which I can engage the full "play" of power and ethics that are involved in each set of encounters. The phrase, "to remove to another place" begins one dictionary definition of translation, (offered in the introductory epigraph), is particularly appropriate for meditations on "transnationalities" – all their between-nesses, movements, border-crossings. Afterall, anthropological fieldwork, and the ethnography it produces, does always move us to "another place."

What might such "dis-placement" mean to the "texts" that are produced especially between women, elite researcher and her subaltern interlocuters? What do these "grassroots texts" suggest about the questions of difference/power/ethics always entailed in such encounters? What can be said about the "collaborative" aspirations involved in revealing the deeply collective nature of all anthropological fieldwork?

Staging the Transnational Plantation, Historically.

First, let us briefly tackle the ethnographic "case" problem by asserting that both the plantation and tea, the commodity that is its raison d'etre, were constituted by deeply historical transnational processes. In the world histories of capitalism and imperial trade this little bit of leaf has played an enormously vivid role: think of the Boston Tea Party, the Chinese trade (which created a balance of payments problem for England) and the Opium Wars (which involved a rather critical triangle trade between Indian opium and Chinese tea). In the heyday of the Chinese tea trade, one third of the East India Company's profits were due to tea. The East India Company was the first and most powerful multinational conglomerate in the world.

The labor of indigenous (adivasi) and Nepali women workers in Indian plantations (set up to battle against the Chinese control of the trade) continued to build the fortunes of the British plantocracy, and tea merchants in India, and then Ceylon. I have explored elsewhere how the "feminized fetishism" of labor and consumption simultaneously, in empire and colony, became vital to the story of tea. This "violence of the fetish" is racially and sexually embodied within the sign of the woman – bent low over the tea bush, or appearing colorfully on the packages which sell tea. Such are the exotic currencies of a star commodity as it circulates in a global and transnational trade.

Second, the "plantation" itself is one of the enduring models of bondage and a catalyst for 'diaspora' in the most profound ways. The dialectical tensions of labor bondage, and the need for labor itself, has given shape to the emergence of both settler colonialism in the Americas as well as the allied impetus for mercantile expansion and commodity trade – through the growing demand for products like sugar, coffee, tea and so on. From slavery to indentureship, from the Americas to Asia and Africa, the "plantation" becomes the crucible of a "diasporic imaginary." This is a crucible created by the brutal, alienating and annihilating waves of human migration in a scale hitherto never seen in world history. Consider the forced horrors of the Middle Passage across the Atlantic, or the coolie ships that plied their indentured cargo from Calcutta to Fiji, Madras to Trinidad, and Bombay to Natal.

Third, let us locate a "transnational" migration within eastern India where these specific stories are located. Let us consider, provisionally, the codes of "nation-ness" to which they might speak. Indeed, what is the "nation" for an adivasi ("original inhabitant"/indigenous) villager who, due to famine, is desperate for food and livelihood? When a kinsman – a sardar (labor contractor) commissioned by British planters desperate for labor – tells her stories of easy cultivation and free plots of land, she goes.

She and her fellow "recruits," as they were known, probably don't understand where this journey as "coolie" batches will lead them. They leave their desh (country, the word that translates closely to the Hindi, "nation") for a place that will become their new "home." This is what the "nation" probably meant to them – that homeland, desh, so suddenly far away. If such a notion of the desh can be viewed as a kind of "protonation," then we might view these labor diasporas as transnational. Simultaneously, labor recruitment from the Kingdom of Nepal also ensured a steady supply of future workers into the Darjeeling hills and the Dooars. Such are the trans-"national" travels in the histories of plantation settlement in eastern India. Translations (and Speaking "Transnationally"): "To Render Into Another Language"(Geddie, 1169)

The tea plantation resonates with a play of tongues, a play that reflects other "nations," other places. It is a polyphony, a cross-cutting chatter of patois and power.

The North Bengal plantation's linguistic diversity is worked through a historical economy in which the procurement and disciplining of women and men into regimes of work constitutes a primary thread of articulation: of utterance, speech, the command over the written word, the many commands over bodies in labor. That is, they speak out the underlying "scripts of power," understood in the broadest sense. The languages spoken flow through the arteries of the plantation system, indexing the ranks of field and factory, coursing through clusters of labor quarters and hutments which make up its villages. It is in these villages, that such a "play of tongues" enters into layered, semi-autonomous planes of social action: community and caste exclusions and inclusions, racialized practices, and gendered rankings speak through the polyvalent chatter of a multilingual landscape.

Let us begin with a mixed, and incomplete list, of what is spoken in a North Bengal plantation: Kurukh (the language of the Oraon), Nepali, Sadri, Bengali, Hindi, Santhali, English. Sadri, a variation of the lingua franca of the Chotanagpur, the homelands of many working communities in the Dooars, is used and understood by all communities. A Nepali woman worker will speak to her Oraon friend in Sadri; a Bengali burra sahib (senior manager) will shout at a Santhali woman for plucking leaf carelessly. Neither speaks his or her "mother-tongue." Sadri, inscribed sometimes into Hindi script, is primarily an oral tradition from the Chotanagpur Plateau.[2] It flows between caste and so-called tribal divisions to create cohesion in what is otherwise a dazzling plural cultural landscape. It acts as social gel within the villages. In other moments of use, as when the planter shouts at a woman worker, Sadri is transformed into a verbal act of command and power.

However, following the caste, class and ethnic patterns of power in North Bengal, Bengali – the mother-tongue of many upper echelon staff and managers – is a primary language of dominance. Significantly, it is not used as commonly as Hindi within regimes of work, because the latter's linguistic markers are more kindred to the lingua franca of the plantation, sadri. However, as the language of the surrounding social and political elite, members of the labor elite –overseers, factory workers, and union leaders – are conversant in the language. Some, particularly union leaders, will serve as political brokers, indeed translators of power, between the planter elite, ordinary workers, and regional political party bosses, most of whom are Bengali.

Bengali also remains the dominant language of instruction in government-run public schools and colleges. The language of education and educational policy in general, continues to exclude Sadri and Nepali speakers in significant ways. On the whole, Sadri speakers would prefer to be instructed in Hindi. While government-run Hindi schools till Class Ten proliferate in the plantation area, the first threshold examination at the end of that class, to gain entrance into junior colleges and for further undergraduate training, is written in Bengali or English. The resulting disenfranchisement of an important sector of the population in North Bengal, which includes non-plantation communities as well, has resulted in serious political unrest and social movements around language issues and educational policy. Despite some campaigns by trade unions and town-based adivasi social organizations, curricular instruction and examination issues have not led to policy shifts within regional educational administration. Because of support from a powerful political movement for ethnic based regional autonomy, the Gorkhaland movement, the Nepali community has been more successful in constructing Nepali-medium schools in the area.

Within the plantation precincts, primary schooling, and the only basic training in literacy that most plantation children will receive, is sparse. In the British period, many schools were run by the plantations but with Indian independence, the government took over its administration. As a result, tea companies do not carry, and seldom exercise, any responsibility around basic education. Curricular instruction is in Hindi, and classes run up to Class Four. Young girls will wait for plantation jobs that they may inherit, if they are lucky, search for casual work, or get married and move into another plantation. If their family has resources and some permanent employment in the plantation, a boy will move into the local Hindi high-school. For the few Catholics and other missionya (Christians), admission to the local Catholic-run schools are a real possibility. Though non-Christian families will also attend these schools, missionya children will be helped by parish priests to gain admission. These schools offer both Hindi and English instruction.

For most women, debates about language policy and basic literacy, and the promise of some upward mobility, is a moot point. However, many remain attentive, and critical, of an educational policy which keeps most of their children from succeeding in higher education, even if they may have the economic resources to educate them beyond Class Ten. Because of customary patriarchal and patrilocal norms of marriage shared by all communities, and because of their potential bodied value as future field-workers, most girls and women are denied basic education. In the classificatory norms of the literacy-education-development paradigm, they are defined as "illiterates." (Freire 1969)

Yet, following Paulo Freire's general contention, that the syntax of the literacy-development paradigm situates those without formal, or text-based, education within a place of essential lack, I will argue that women are the primary translators of the historical and cultural knowledges of the plantation. (Freire 1969) Theirs is a polyphonic oral mastery of a knowledge base that they reproduce, critique and create anew in their kitchens, rituals and fields of labor. Though marginalized from the formal educational system and from socio-economic mobility, theirs is a cultural literacy that cannot be defined by lack. Certainly, the conditions leading to non-literacy radically diminishes the chance of socio-economic betterment and upward mobility, but it is not a primary sign of their sense of social being. Indeed, their remarkable facility with languages, in various sites of power, constitutes an ontology of personhood, and sociality, which is necessary, powerful and creative.

In important ways, their subordination within the plantation system necessitates their knowledges of what are the dominant languages of rule: Bengali, Hindi, and even a smattering of English. This is in addition to Sadri, Nepali, and perhaps the old mother-tongues of their homelands in the Chotanagpur. Munnu Kujoor who understands four languages and speaks two (Nepali and Sadri) fluently, is Oraon. Her language is Kurukh which, she tells me, is still spoken in the Purana (Old) Line, one of the villages where many Oraons live. "It is not like Hindi, didi (elder sister), the words are totally different. You know, like the inter-menter that they speak in south India. Have you heard Tamil bhasa (language)? I think it sounds like that. I don't speak it but my parents could."

I speak to Munnu Kujoor in a basic colloquial Hindi/Bengali mix. My own education in an international English-medium school in northern Nigeria and India, and subsequent undergraduate and graduate education in the United States, has resulted in linguistic loss. It is typical of a certain bourgeois, postcolonial and diasporic experience.

Taught Hindi until Class Ten, and with enough skills to write in simple Hindi, I have adequate conversational skills in that language. I was never taught to write in Bengali, my mother-tongue, though speak it better than Hindi. I learned early that the loss of literate facility in my mother-tongue, marked me as firanghi (foreign) even before I had left India for higher education.

However, ironically, such a loss of literate privilege enabled me to enter the oral worlds of women in important ways. Indeed, they recognized that while I embodied upper-caste, upper-class privilege, my broken facility with both dominant languages of rule (including my own mother-tongue) resulted in an awkwardness that they could help me with as I searched for a word from Bengali to translate into Hindi. It was an awkwardness that made me enter the "outside" places of linguistic belonging.

Certainly, their confidence in various linguistic traditions was more significant than my self-conscious search for the "correct" syntax and linguistic useage in two. Though my English marked clearly the privileges of Amriki-ness (American-ness), and the ultimate sahib-language[3], those quick shifts between Hindi-Bengali-Hindi created the necessary patois of communication – one which I, in some embarrassment, called my kichdi bhasa (mixed-curry language).

Such are the vagaries and possibilities of translation of experience to language: of scripted loss, reaching beyond worlds into new kinds of words and arrangements, a calligraphy of what is spoken, what is wrenched from memory, what is not said. The presumed intimacy that my knowledge of Hindi could bring to bear to our basic communication was always fractured, but it was a fracturing that created other forms of connection. Loss was also, in this instance, possibility.

Simultaneously, let us not forget how these movements between languages, and the new languages created, constitute a new kind of trans-understanding. This sketch reinvigorates our understandings of the dazzling pluralities of linguistic mix which continue to 'remember' the other places – the desh – many left, never knowing whether they would get back, or where they were going.

Authorship: "Conversion, Paraphrase, Version, Transformation, Change, Rendition" (Microsoft Word 2000 Thesarus, U.S. Version)

> Make Something and Show Us
> Everyone thinks I am illiterate.
> I am going to be an author and show them.
> Everyone thinks I am incapable of anything.
> I will do something and show them.
> Everyone thinks I am bad.
> I will show them by doing good.
> Everyone thinks I am the land's grass.
> I will show that I am the sky's stars.
> Everyone thinks I don't have a mind.
> I will show them that I am a poet.
> Rita Chhetri (10-3-99)

Rita Chhetri writes this poem as part of a collection of essays, poems, and testimonials that she has been collecting for some years. She works at Debpara Tea Estate, a plantation neighboring the plantation which is my primary fieldsite, New Dooars Tea Estate. We met first in 1993 but have started a conversation about her writing only in

1998. She writes from her memory of an alphabet learned last in Class Five, the extent of her participation in formal education. Because of her family's small resources, her brother continued his education while she took permanent employment as a tea plucker. She keeps loose pages in a thick cardboard folder, in a plastic bag, so that the monsoon rains which seep through the ceiling of her labor quarter, her home, do not damage the papers.

When we meet again in 1998, after a five year hiatus, she tells me that she has never lost her fire for writing; that she wrote on any scrap of paper, even the scratch paper used to make packets of channa (snacks). I asked her whether she kept these scraps, stained by the residue of lemon juice and spices, and she nodded, "some, but many times I would rip them up and throw them away. I was so angry, so angry…" I asked to see some of her saved work and told her to keep collecting whatever she wrote, that one day I would try and help to turn them into a book.

We sit together on some monsoon days in the summer of 2000, talking about a collaborative project in which her writing might be produced in situ, as a book. After xeroxing her work so we each have separate copies of her writing, we work on translations. She writes in Nepali, in Hindi script. I don't understand Nepali so she translates each line into Bengali, and sometimes Hindi words that I might understand. Since I can read the Hindi, we read each line out together. I scribble out initial translations of each line in English, repeating them back to her in Bengali. It is a long process and she does not have much time to offer away from household and labor responsibilities.

The poem presented is dated as being written on March 10, 1999. She tells me she wrote it as a response to a man's mockery of a small sewing business she had begun with a few unemployed women in the plantations. She says, "He mocked me and said, 'how do you think you will run this? You don't even know how to read and write." I want to give it to this man who said this to me. I want to give him a book." Complicities (Marcus, 1997).

Rita Chhetri's poem, the conditions of her writing and her translating some to me, begs a scrutiny of another politics of translation – not only the process of "conventional" translation as sketched above but the translation of this encounter and experience into an ethnographic text. The specific translation of her written Nepali into English, and into this particular text of English, is an act that transforms the enabling effects of oral dialogue (Rita speaking her meaning and intent to me in Hindi/Bengali) into a language, congealed into text, that she will not read, and which will circulate in article book-form, across other borderlines of power.

I will offer only some of her written samples as breaks, or punctuations of a dream which I envision about some women-led community organizing efforts taking place in the area. Though we plan to work on an entirely separate project which will make her, singularly, an author, this possible collaboration will depend on more consistent meetings. The book never happens, though we end up collaborating[4] in grassroots organizing from 1999–2007, a collaboration that is equally fragile and burdened by the messy ethics of inequality of status and power between us.

The aspirations around this collaboration of book production and authorship is mediated through a politics of value: time, wages-lost, bodied energies. Its immediate political economy will depend on how she can get time "away" from her necessary wage-labor and how we can both ensure that she incurs no losses, material or otherwise. These are sets of tricky ethical calculations and need to be underscored within any narrative claims of ethnographic collaboration. In the few days she spends with me discussing her writing, she takes hours from her weekly holiday to meet. Though she does not lose daily wages in this process, she does give me time that she might spend in household chores. These hours offer a bit of rest, she assures me. With the usual ambivalences, I learn to accept her will and her desire to spend time sharing her other work.

Within this preliminary stage of narrative presentation, I appropriate her "voice" for a specific kind of analysis about translation. It is a task of translation and insertion, which is central to ethnographic production. Yet, despite its fragmentations and its reflexivities, the future ethnography cannot escape the issues of ethical accountability to one's interlocuters and to the analysis produced. Claims of textual transparency through self-referential moments around ethnographic collaboration, and efforts of collaboration within actual social practice are connected within a political, epistemological arc that should show these faultlines of inequality clearly.

Let me ask you, then, to revisit the place within which Rita and I are sutured into a particular web of social power. Beyond the actual symbol of languages we inscribe into our rough and lined paper, our encounter folds into another page about the neo-feudal politics of rural India. It is one that inscribes, continuously and consistently, our politics of location: her Nepali working class and gendered personhood; my Bengali upper-caste, bourgeois self, connected by kinships of class privilege to the postcolonial plantocracy, and far-flung cosmopolitan diasporas. Our encounter crosses certain boundaries of power, but also underlines those terms of inequality. These are oppositional positions.

My act of "appropriation" is, let's push it further, also an act of thievery even as I expose the faultlines of our encounter. As Jigna Desai, Danielle Bouchard and Diane Detournay suggest at the end of their essay on transnational feminist praxis, "admitting one's culpabilities and naming the transaction as stealing allows for "honorability."5 (Desai et al., 51–52) In other words, the assertion that epistemological claims of the text itself are implicated in the snarls of accountability and ethics within field encounters is now a given, but perhaps we need to push into the ethical questions a bit more, start tracing out something we might imagine as a system of ethical-narrative-accountability.

"Honorable thievery" might be one way to thread these forms of epistemic violence – that which is "done" to make this "text" come into being. In that light, self-referencing, reflexivity and postmodern textual strategies are not being used here as a magic trick, a sleight of hand that might actually obscure the more obvious terms of feudal power that define relationships in a North Bengal plantation. It is not intended to obscure the fact that the act of translation, like any act of power, begs for an honest web of ethical accountability.

Why did I think, when first stepping into the Labor Lines in 1991 that here was something kindred to apartheid? Why did I think that we, postcolonial sahibs and memsahibs, wore (to paraphrase Franz Fanon) Brown Masks? Any claims of "transnational sisterhood" from such epistemic sites have to be made, then, very carefully. Yet, the politics of claim, however, might not be the same as the politics of the imagination – the imagination can embrace these faultlines, the thieving, and still stretch towards fragile solidarities. These kinships, unlike liberal understandings of "sisterhood," begin with the undeniable recognition of structural power. Understanding intention, hers and mine, is important in this recognition for it allows the possibility of encounter. But it is always sutured tightly to the nets of privilege and subalternity which fling us in opposing directions.

But I am still hopeful about the possibilities that can seed within transnational feminist imaginaries. When the imagination remains in dialectical connection to the bodied and the immediate, others possible kinships (containing the tensions and fissures within) might be crafted. The maw of representational politics do not need to stop us from imagining, dreaming and acting.

I don't think of this consciously when Rita and I sit, trying to thread together some common language of understanding. I don't think of this consciously when I try to find her in the hospital where she works as a nurse's aide, many years after I met her in plantation country. Will she remember me? Our "relationship" is fractured by territorial and temporal distance. Our sessions, sometimes a few days long, are interrupted by her work demands, my other research and organizing efforts, and the inevitable departures to Calcutta and California. Does she experience these interruptions, particularly the long absences, as a certain betrayal? Does she weigh my rhetorics about such textual, and other, possibilities with caution?

These are reflections, now translated in California, born from privileged travel, a cosmopolitan migration. There is only some sharp historical irony when she tells me of how two generations ago; her kinsmen came here from the harsh slopes of the Nepal Himalayas in search of work. Some went to Darjeeling, some came to Dooars. These are not co-eval travels. I do not imagine them as such.

Patriarchal Recordings: "the automatic re-transmission of a telegraphic message." (Geddie, 1169)

It is late 1992, well into the first year of fieldwork. I have bought a small tape recorder and mini-cassettes though am hesitant to use the machine. To use it feels more extractive than conversations (which I have without taking notes), and I don't want to jeopardize the fragile trust of the few women who have befriended me. But I am also keen on hearing life stories, in detail, and though I take notes at night, trying to remember what was said from memory, I often forget details – a turn of phrase or a sigh. Finally, I mention this to Munnu Kujoor, an Oraon woman-worker with whom I have a consistently close relationship. She has told me of the songs that women sing while in the field, as they pluck the tea. I would like to hear these songs, and perhaps even tape them. I tell Munnu that I will give her the tape recorder and she can decide, with the women, what they would like to say. She asks her dol (labor gang) about this and they agree but ask that I not accompany Munnu into the tea field. She tells me that they will feel inhibited and shy. The subsequent recordings are hilarious: songs, fragments of songs interspersed with dialogue about the crazy memsahib's project. I transcribe some but have never published these.

Munnu keeps the tape recorder with her and she tells me that she uses it at night, speaking into it like a daily journal. She asks that I don't ever write it down, that it is between her and me. I listen to some of what she shares, we talk about it and I never transcribe it. Then, one day she tells me that she has been speaking to a Nepali woman in her natal village and she wanted to speak into the tape recorder, give me her life story. Munnu says, "She has had a very hard life, didi, (elder sister) you have to hear it: her father beat her, her husband is terrible. He is a drunkard and beats her. She lost many children and she works and works despite everything. She knows many things about history too. She wants to speak to you." Delighted at this opportunity to meet someone who actually wants to talk to me, and also into the tape recorder, we make arrangements to meet. I ask Munnu repeatedly if it will be okay to take the tape recorder with me. She knows that people suspect I work for the U.S. or Indian government, that I am considered a spy, so I insist that she clear this again with her friend. I am told that all is well. One late afternoon, we head over to the little liquor shop which her friend, Maya, runs with her husband. Maya, Munnu and I go up a rickety flight of stairs to a small room in the store itself. We are introduced, I give Maya the tape recorder, show her how to start and stop the machine and tell her that if at any moment she feels uncomfortable with the process, she can turn it off, and also that I will give her the tape.

She says she is excited to tell the story because "we women have been too long under the men's feet and Munnu has explained why you are here." Though I am not expecting this moment of proto-feminist analysis, the three of us begin a discussion about women's status in the villages and in plantation work. It is a sharp and exciting discussion. After about fifteen minutes, I hear some shouting downstairs and then a wiry Nepali man bursts into the room. Maya's husband has arrived.

He shouts at Maya, glares at me with anger, and grabs the tape recorder. "What is going on, memsahib," he shouts, "how dare you come here to talk to my wife with this?" I stumble into an explanation, apologizing profusely while Munnu and Maya look aghast. I explain to him that I am interested in "women's stories" and that is all and Munnu had said it would be okay to do so. I know, instinctively, that I cannot mention Maya's keen interest in our meeting. Munnu lives in another plantation and members of her family in this, her natal plantation village, are also powerful union members. Munnu also tries to placate him. Finally, I ask him to listen to what his wife has said. It is clear to me that if he does not, she might be harmed. Thankfully, she has spoken generally about the plantation, and had not yet begun to share any of her own personal predicament. As he rewinds the tape, I realize, with some horror, that I am using an old cassette which I had tested earlier and had an acquaintance speak into. As luck would have it, Maya's husband started the tape as this acquaintance said in English: "I am the son of a judge." Hearing the English, Maya's husband lost his equilibrium again and this time he was shaking with anxiety: "Who is this speaking in English? Where is the "judge"?" Once again, we placated him. He asked me bluntly which government I was spying for. He told me that he was a trade union leader, as well as a field overseer, and that I must now come and speak to his union about what I was doing in the plantation. I told him I would be happy to talk to the entire union about what I was doing because I had nothing to hide. Then with some dramatic flourish, I took the cassette out of the recorder and handed it to him. I said, "Look, I have no intent of taking something away that upsets you so. Please be assured that I won't do this again and keep the cassette." We set up an appointment with the union leaders and I left with Munnu. Maya kept her eyes down as she said goodbye.

The attempt to "get" a woman's life story, in a collaborative way (through a friend of hers) was ended summarily in a dramatic moment of patriarchal disruption. It was an important "failure" on several levels, but in that moment of non-fruition, (of the narrative interrupted, of the narrative-that-could-not-be told) much can be learned about the politics of translation.

First, it underscored the problematic nature and use of machines in "getting" a narrative. Certainly, Maya's husband may have viewed her "captured talk" as revealing his treatment of her. But he was most explicitly incensed, and troubled, by the English fragment which suggested the power of a state, which might capriciously rule his life. Indeed, his recognition of the English word "judge" suggests recognition of a distant, but present, governing apparatus. In his eyes, I was certainly a representative of a ruling elite, and language, which organized plantation feudalisms. That moment of machined error revealed the highly problematic, and complex, ways that the oral is "caught" into text. Though I had given Maya the tape recorder, it was still read as a tool of the state, and also a certain colonizing access to their lives.

Second, my deferral to him (in effusive apology) might have been read by Maya, and Munnu, as an acquiescence to his bullying, and indeed, the blatant patriarchal interruption of a fragile feminized solidarity that was coming into play. Since we had met to discuss, among other things, the subordination of women, my easy capitulation to his anger may have been read more ambiguously by the two other women. However, at that moment of rupture, I perceived the dangerous effects of my own gendered privilege upon them. Though I explained to Munnu why I had not responded to his bullying, I was left with a nagging feeling that she thought I had capitulated too easily.

Third, I recognized – yet again – how fragile moments of a proto-feminist solidarity, and intimacy, can easily collapse into the maw of ethical failure. Munnu had told me that Maya was regularly beaten by this man – why did I not insist that we meet in a safer, private place? Did I jeopardize her physical safety despite the fact that I turned everything over to him? Though Munnu assured me that Maya was fine, I was left with a nagging sense that I should have never come with that tape recorder.

Certainly, this small incident can be read in other ways too: The fact is that both Munnu and Maya knowingly invited me to speak with her; the fact is that they wanted to speak into the recorder in a collective and powerful way. Despite my own ambivalences, I cannot deny their agency, the force of their conscious will.

The fact of patriarchal disruption offers, again, a moment of surrender to the immediate experience – to recognize that the interruption of one woman's attempt to speak her life presented a powerful narrative about ethnographic "failure." If the session with Maya had been taped without interruption, the choices of transcription and translation would have opened other kinds of questions. In this instance, I learn again that many lessons are cohered in the tasks of translation. In those moments of rupture, I need to abandon myself to these lessons, and to the shadow of the narrative aborted.

Conclusion: Messy Braids.

Feminist anthropologists have explored, for some time now, the ethics and geopolitics of representation in a discipline founded on colonial expansion and its knowledges. Following their critical scholarship and lead, through these "grassroots texts," I reveal some faultlines of power which mediate the production of ethnographic narratives. From the outset of fieldworks, these texts were catalyzed by a basic feminist desire to highlight plantation women's lives, experiences and "voices." In both these episodes, there was an attempt at "collaboration" (in the dialogical process of creating the narratives, through writing and recording). Certainly, both episodes offer the "collective" and "dialogical" moments at the center of the process.

In the encounter with Rita Chetri, I begin with an assertion of voice which quickly demonstrates her astute and critical sensibilities: a moving example of one subaltern woman's claim to authorship, to the power of writing itself. Indeed, I was eager to translate Rita's collection but never managed to do so, for reasons that were "transnational" as much as they were about the fissures of social status and material power which separated us. It also involved grassroots organizing that took off from 1999, that engaged our energies and our "collaborations in other ways. But that is another, linked story, beside the immediate concerns of this essay.

Our encounters offer a flickering attempt at "collaboration" in the production of text, which does not really come to fruition. I still have copies of all her material – translated into English but cannot get myself to publish them as an example of innovative fieldwork collaboration, and a feminist text of plantation subalternity. This refusal is already a refusal of "power" – Rita simply does not have the access to put her work forward in the circuits of written, print capital. I refuse to broker her words and this creates a tangle, a set of knottings, which I need to attend to with more ethical nuance. For now, the ethical issues – which also include a eight year old relationship around organizing which also fractured badly– means that the copies of her stories and poem rest on a dusty shelf.

In the second episode I shared involving Munnu, Maya, and Maya's anxious and disruptive husband, I offer a "ruptural moment' that appears most obvious in terms of the "impossibilities" of the narrative. Yet, what interests me here is that the sense of ethical "failure" can be seen in more nuanced ways. Indeed, this sense of "failure" of 'getting' Maya's story was in my inability to "lift" what she wanted "displaced" – relayed – to others. That is, her tale of endurance and perhaps resistance to patriarchal violence. But I was also learning sharp lessons about the deeper context of the plantation, and the scrutiny of planters and union leaders as I meandered through these spaces and spoke, primarily, to women workers. My quick capitulation to the husband's intimidation also had everything to do with the pedagogies of isolation in which my own gender and status was so definitively marked by the geopolitics of privilege as an insider/outsider, regionally and transnationally. More importantly, I did not try to meet her again because of my concern that my presence had already made her more vulnerable to intimate violence. That remained the final punctuation for the story that never-made-it, but which also birthed another one.

Through exploring these difficult issues of power and ethics within ethnographic production, (and narrative-making) I have also sought to create a capacious space within which i/we can call out the plural and the paradoxical, the difficult and the joyous in all our epistemic work – and everything in-between as well. Perhaps we can create an unbounded space using our "transnational feminist imaginaries," – a liminal zone, crafted (and freed) by ethical and honest critiques and the belief in the importance of solidarities that can still be built across the crevasses of power and difference which separate us. Here. There. Here.

Notes

1 My involvement with plantation communities and politics started in the early 1990s'with my more conventional field research phase in the early 1990's. This shifted to grassroots organizing from 1999- 2007. The small narratives of "ethnographic rupture" that I share in this essay come from the early phase of fieldwork, not from the direct experience of organizing.

2 Sadri, also known as sadhani, is a patois used in the Chotanagpur Plateau by diverse and distinct linguistic adivasi and caste-communities. I surmise that this is a kind of bridge-language that combines aspects of several other languages in this highly plural linguistic landscape.

3 By this phrasing, I merely gesture to the urban-elite English spoken in some manager's (sahib's) parlours. Increasingly, though, this "public school" Indian English is being replaced by managers who are more comfortable with Hindi or Bengali.

4 It is important here to flag the problematic of "collaboration" which can assume co-evalness. I am suggesting something far more problematically nuanced and unequal. Other authors in this excellent collection also parse out the claims and problematic of collaboration in very similar ways to what I am attempting in this brief essay.

5 Jigna Desai, Danielle Bouchard and Diane Detournay use the work of Helen Hoy to offer this very important line of thinking. Helen Hoy looks at the "collaborations between Metis Canadian artist, activist and writer Maria Campbell and white Canadian performer and writer Linda Griffiths and her own production of scholarship on Native Canadian literature as a white woman … as maybe framed by stealing." P.61–62.

References

Desai, Jigna, Danielle Bouchard, and Diane Detournay. "Disavowed Legacies and Honorable Thievery: The work of the "Transnational" in Feminist and LGBTQ Studies." Critical Transnational Feminist Praxis. Eds. Amanda Lock Swarr and Richa Nagar. Albany: SUNY Press 2010. 46–62. Print.

Freire, Paulo. Pedagogy of the Oppressed. Trans. Myra Bergman Ramos. New York: Herder and Herder, 1970; New York: Continuum, 2001.

Geddie, William. Ed. Chambers Twentieth Century Dictionary. London, Edinburgh: W.&R. Chambers, 1901.

Karamcheti, Indira. "Aimé Césaire's Subjective Geographies: Translating Place and the Difference It Makes." Between Languages and Cultures: Translation and Cross-Cultural Texts. Eds. Anuradha Dingwaney and Carol Maier. Pittsburgh: University of Pittsburgh Press 1995. 181–197.

Marcus, George. "The Uses of Complicity in the Changing Mis-en-Scene of Anthropological Fieldwork."Representations 59 (Summer 1997), 85–107.

Mohanty, Chandra. 1986. "Under Western Eyes: Feminist Scholarship and Colonial Discourses." Boundary 2 XII/XIII (1, 3): 333–358. Print.

Nagar, Richa and Amanda Lock Swarr. "Introduction: Theorizing Transnational Feminist Praxis." Critical Transnational Feminist Praxis. Eds. Amanda Lock Swarr and Richa Nagar. Albany: SUNY Press 2010. 1–20. Print.

Index

Page numbers in **Bold** represent figures.